MW00682013

# HOW TO
# MANAGE
# STRESS
# FOR
# SUCCESS

## The WorkSmart Series

# HOW TO MANAGE STRESS FOR SUCCESS

## Sara Zeff Geber

**amacom**

AMERICAN MANAGEMENT ASSOCIATION
THE WORKSMART SERIES

New York • Atlanta • Boston • Chicago • Kansas City • San Francisco • Washington, D.C.
Brussels • Toronto • Mexico City

This book is available at a special
discount when ordered in bulk quantities.
For information, contact Special Sales Department,
AMACOM, a division of American Management Association,
135 West 50th Street, New York, NY 10020.

This publication is designed to provide accurate and authoritative information in regard to the subject matter covered. It is sold with the understanding that the publisher is not engaged in rendering legal, accounting, or other professional service. If legal advice or other expert assistance is required, the services of a competent professional person should be sought.

Library of Congress Cataloging-in-Publication Data

Geber, Sara Zeff.
    How to manage stress for success / Sara Zeff Geber.
        p.    cm.—(The WorkSmart series)
    Includes bibliographical references.
    ISBN 0-8144-7840-9
    1.  Stress management.    I.  Series.
RA785.G43    1996
155.9'042—dc20                                95-52832
                                                  CIP

© 1996 AMACOM, a division of
American Management Association, New York
All rights reserved.
Printed in the United States of America.

This publication may not be reproduced,
stored in a retrieval system,
or transmitted in whole or in part,
in any form or by any means, electronic,
mechanical, photocopying, recording, or otherwise,
without the prior written permission of AMACOM,
a division of American Management Association,
135 West 50th Street, New York, NY 10020.

Printing number

10   9   8   7   6   5   4   3   2   1

To my father, **Leo**
Always my inspiration and guide

# CONTENTS

# PART

# I

# LOOKING BACKWARD

# What Is Stress and Why Do I Have It?

The facts are startling: Stress has surpassed the common cold as the most prevalent health problem in the United States. Between 80 percent and 90 percent of industrial accidents have been related to emotional problems. Stress-related injuries account for more than 70 percent of all absenteeism, and the loss to the gross national product from this drop in productivity is estimated to be nearly 10 percent. The American Institute of Stress calculates that stress-related illness costs the American economy $100 billion per year. Productivity losses are estimated at $17 billion annually.

The insurance industry has calculated that stress-related disability claims have more than doubled during the last decade. This is passed on to the consumer as increased costs for coverage. The combined financial impact (increased costs plus lost productivity) on corporate America is a staggering $68 billion annually.

More important than statistics and corporate financial health, however, is the impact that our life-in-the-fast-lane is having on our own personal health, our relationships with those we love, and our spiritual and emotional well-being. This book takes a comprehensive look at the psychological and physiological phenomenon of stress, where stress comes from and what it does to us, and the role played by modern society.

Part I focuses on a general understanding of stress and provides the reader with an opportunity to assess its impact and manifestations in his/her own life. Part II takes the reader forward from understanding to action. The focus is on changing the stressful elements in our lives, our perception of them, and/or the ways in which we cope.

The book is designed to be several things: information, guidance, workbook, action plan, and opportunity for real introspection. What it is *not* designed to be is a sermon. So before you begin to read, promise yourself that you will not use this book as an excuse to punish yourself. Everyone who reads it has a little to a lot of stress in their lives. It comes with the package of living these days. What you do about it is no one's business but yours. You may even *like* it; many people thrive on stress. Wherever you are, it's okay. It's also okay to do something about it. And it's okay to do nothing about it until you're ready, or ever! It's your life; it's your choice. Enjoy it.

# CHAPTER 1

## WHAT IS STRESS?

**"Stress is the Spice of Life; the absence of stress is death."**

**—HANS SELYE**

Stress has been defined in many ways by many different people. It has been a topic of interest to medical professionals, social scientists, anthropologists, psychologists, and even zoologists. For our purposes, it seems most enlightening to examine it from several different perspectives, thereby getting a broad overview of the phenomenon, as well as its roots in the history of humankind.

Any discussion of stress surely would be incomplete without some mention of the work of Hans Selye, M.D. Considered by many to be the father of stress research, Selye began studying the phenomenon of stress over fifty years ago. His classic and still widely respected work, *The Stress of Life,* first published in 1946, gave us this definition: Stress is a *nonspecific response of the body to a demand.* It is still recognized today as the simplest and best physiological definition of what happens within our bodies when we are knocked out of our comfortable equilibrium.

Looking a little deeper into the mechanics of this phenomenon, we find that the physiological stress reaction is our body's response to any change, threat, or pressure put upon it—from outside forces or from within. Our body then tries to regain its normal state and protect itself from potential harm. Thousands of years ago, during a far less structured and complex era, individuals needed this response to stay alive and combat various kinds of physical threats (animals, other humans, flood, fire). This is one of many unique ways in which homo sapiens are equipped to survive in the world. The purpose of stress, then, is to keep us alive and healthy!

Today, much of the stress we experience is manufactured in our minds. We perceive a threat (loss of job, anger from spouse, not meeting a deadline), and we begin to worry. Our bodies, lacking the ability to discern a deadline from a hairy beast, still react in much the same way they did 4,000 years ago.

**Stress is inevitable. To be entirely without stress is to be dead!**

Stress is inevitable. To be entirely without stress is to be dead! However, not all stress is unpleasant. Selye distinguished between pleasant stress, which he labeled *eustress,* and unpleasant stress, or *distress*. When we discuss stress today, we are usually referring to distress, but we can all relate to pleasant situations or occurrences that have caused us stress: weddings, births, promotions, receiving awards, reuniting with old friends, and countless others. Any change, positive or negative, requires a response from our bodies in order to adapt and bring us back to our relatively peaceful state.

We also can look at stress as a state of imbalance between demands (from inside *or* outside sources) and our perceived abilities to meet those demands. This is experienced most acutely when the expectation is that the consequences of

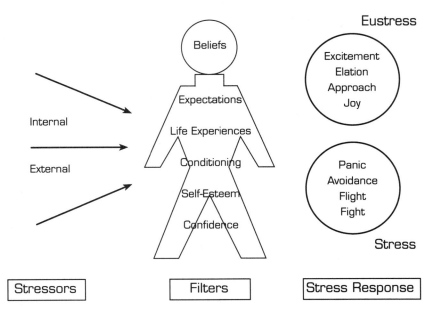

meeting the demand will be quite different from the consequences of *not* meeting the demand. For example, if you were asked to create a marketing brochure and you felt confident of your knowledge of the product and your ability to organize the information, create attractive graphics, and put an interesting and attractive spin on the information, you would find the whole experience far less stressful than if you considered yourself inadequately informed, a poor writer, and not particularly creative. It would be doubly stressful if, on top of the pressure for an eye-popping masterpiece, the initial recipients were to be a beta-test group of the company's largest and most valued customers, who would be asked to give feedback on their reactions to the new product based on your marketing piece.

## STRESSORS

The stress response is ignited by a stressor. Some common stressors include:

- Physical threats
- Threats to our self-image
- An important life event
- A fight or conflict with a friend/relative/coworker
- Tight deadlines
- Loss of something or someone we care for

Stressors can be any kind of stimulation, internal or external, that triggers the physiological stress response. But here we begin to see individual differences. In order for an event to be labeled a stressor, it needs to be *perceived* as one. A request from your spouse to pick up a prescription at the drugstore may be perceived as a completely reasonable task and fit right in with other errands for that day (nonstressful). However, it may require considerable juggling of an already full schedule and cause some bad feelings or an argument between you and your spouse (stressful).

Like stress itself, stressors come in two varieties: *distressors* and *eustressors*. An opportunity to stand up at a meeting and say a few words may be perceived as scary, threatening, or risky for one individual, but a second individual may have been expecting or hoping to be called upon and may see it as an opportunity to appear knowledgeable and intelligent. The first sees the situation as a distressor, the second as a eustressor, or positive challenge.

# THEORIES ABOUT STRESS

## Type A vs. Type B Personalities

Since the 1970s, one of the most popular theories about stress and our health has been that of cardiologists Meyer Friedman and Ray Rosenman. They observed two vastly different behavior types among their patients. One kind of behavior, Type A, they found much more likely to lead to heart attacks in otherwise healthy individuals. People exhibiting Type B behavior, however, were less likely to end up in a hospital bed with heart problems.

### Distinguishing Characteristics of the Two Types of Behavior

| Type A | Type B |
| --- | --- |
| • Moves quickly. | • Moves unhurriedly. |
| • Eats fast. | • Eats peacefully. |
| • Speaks rapidly. | • Speaks slowly. |
| • Frequently feels impatient. | • Is patient. |
| • Is aggressive and competitive at work. | • Is cooperative and collaborative at work. |
| • Is very time-conscious. | • Is not time-driven, sometimes late. |
| • Is easily upset or angered. | • Is easy-going. |
| • Is highly motivated to achieve. | • Is generally satisfied. |
| • Is perceived as strong and forceful. | • Is soft-spoken, laid back. |

| Type A | Type B |
| --- | --- |
| • Feels restless during periods of inactivity. <br> • Frequently tries to do multiple tasks at once. | • Enjoys leisure and quiet time. <br> • Does one task at a time. |

Type A's often achieve phenomenal career success and a great deal of recognition for their efforts. However, the physical and emotional toll may be quite high. Along with a coronary heart disease rate that Friedman and Rosenman found to be seven times that of Type B's, Type A's are rarely satisfied with what they accomplish. So they drive themselves harder and harder, pushing other people away as a consequence. And Type A behavior is not limited to work and career. Type A's report less satisfaction with family and other relationships, as well, further alienating those close to them. This might lead us to conclude that the saying "it's lonely at the top" may have more to do with alienation and provocation than it does with a mere pyramid of numbers.

## Person-Environment Fit

Another popular theory about stress is the Person-Environment (P-E) Fit Theory, developed at the Institute for Social Research. The focus of this theory is the relationship between an individual's *perception* of a task, his perception of his *ability* to complete that task, and his *motivation* to complete the task. The hypothesis is that feelings of stress should increase as the P-E gap widens. Findings indicate that this is in fact the case and that stress varies as a function of level of challenge (stress) preferred by the individual.

Let's take an example. Some engineers are challenged by long hours, a fast pace, and a chaotic atmosphere. They enjoy the feeling of importance that comes with being a big fish in a small pond where lots of people depend on them. And they don't particularly mind letting their job take priority over everything else in their life. Small, newly formed, start-up companies need to look for such individuals in order to create a good person-environment fit. These engineers will thrive in that kind of climate.

In contrast, if the president of a small start-up company decides to recruit engineers with a good reputation and track record from IBM, she may soon discover that she has some very stressed-out people on her hands. Individuals who thrive in a large stable environment often do poorly in chaos. It creates a level of stress for them that is often intolerable. The same is true in reverse. An entrepreneurial engineer will feel stifled, unmotivated, and out of place in a traditional, slow-moving company.

## COPING TECHNIQUES

Stress is cumulative. Our bodies are well equipped to deal with a reasonable amount of stress throughout our lives. However, as we explore in Chapter 6, our world is becoming more and more complex and demanding. It is particularly important today, and will become increasingly critical in future decades, to make sure we have adequate coping techniques to manage our stressful lives.

Coping techniques are thought patterns and behavioral habits that neutralize stressors or mitigate their impact on us. When we receive a poor review at work, our thoughts often focus on ideas like "my manager didn't really have an adequate opportunity to observe how hard I worked" or "my supervisor just doesn't value nontechnical skills." You've probably called these thoughts *rationalizations*. That's exactly what they are; rationalizing is a coping mechanism. (They're much easier to see when others are doing it!)

Coping is our effort to manage the demands we perceive as negative. Human beings automatically develop complex coping mechanisms; it's part of the socialization and maturation process. These coping mechanisms differ widely from one individual to another. And they range from trivial to severe.

At the extreme or severe end is what psychiatrists call *repression*. When something truly devastating happens in life, especially when it occurs at a young age, our minds may simply destroy all record of it in a desperate effort to maintain normalcy. The memory becomes unavailable to the conscious mind. You could compare it to pressing the "delete" key on your computer to wipe out a file. Much has been written lately about repressed memories with regard to childhood sexual abuse. That is the kind of severe trauma that can cause full repression.

At the milder end of the spectrum are unconscious coping strategies like moving slower on a hot day or staying in bed when we don't feel very well. We also engage in many deliberate coping activities like putting cotton in our ears to work in a noisy room, cuddling with the dog or cat when we feel lonely or unloved, or taking a long bubble bath after a trying day.

Sometimes we must supplement these everyday coping mechanisms in order to meet elevated demands. The fact that you are reading this book may mean you are currently experiencing increased demands in your life. In Part II, we explore a great variety of ways in which you can enhance your ability to cope. You may want to supplant old ways with new ones, or simply try some new techniques for awhile.

## SATISFACTION

One final element completes our big-picture understanding of the nature of stress: its mirror image, *satisfaction*. Stress and satisfaction often operate like a teeter-totter; when one goes up the other goes down. But this is not always the case. It is possible for someone to have high stress *and* high satisfaction, if they have a feeling of control and choice in the situation and have functional coping mechanisms. It is not as likely, however, that someone with low satisfaction also would have low stress. Generally, feelings of discontent or dissatisfaction go hand-in-hand with high levels of stress. In Chapter 3 you have an opportunity to assess your satisfaction level.

# CHAPTER 2

## WHERE DOES OUR STRESS COME FROM?

Our stress comes from two sources: inside our body or mind (internal) and outside of ourselves (external).

## INTERNAL STRESSORS

Our internal stressors involve both our biology and our personality.

### Biology

Some of us are more productive in the morning hours, preferring to awaken before dawn to start work early. Others feel their peak of productivity in the afternoon or even late at night. These biological energy cycles (called Circadian rhythms) seem to play a role in our experience of stress.

> "People are not disturbed by things, but by the view they take of them.
>
> —EPICTETUS

At one time it was thought that the fairest method for scheduling shift work was a rotation where the less desirable second and third shifts didn't always fall on the same people. Most companies have abandoned that practice in favor of letting people choose their shift, to the extent possible, and remain there until they desire a change. At airline reservation centers, those late-night shifts are often selected by the most senior agents. Interviews with third-, or "graveyard-," shift workers produce a picture of someone who functions best late at night.

Those who function best late in the day are sometimes referred to as "night people." Likewise, the early riser is occasionally referred to as a "morning person." Night people often find early morning work very stressful because the energy level they need to perform optimally is just not available to them at that hour. It is a poor person-environment fit. The same is true of a newly hired "morning person" who must start out on an evening shift until there is a daytime shift opening.

In addition, some of us are more prone genetically to specific diseases, allergies, and disabilities. These maladies and illnesses upset our equilibrium, sap our strength, and make it more difficult to function at our desired level. When we are ill, our bodies are hard at work trying to restore equilibrium. They have little energy left to perform everyday tasks. A sick person is a stressed person, in the purest sense of the word.

Circadian rhythms and genetic makeup are static phenomena in our lives; we can do very little to change them. But we can do a great deal to counteract their influence on our health by improving other internal factors such as fitness and nutrition.

## Personality

"The most powerful— and the most controllable— stressor in the world is the human mind."

—MATTESON AND IVANCEVICH

Each one of us is unique in how we experience the world and how others experience us. Our feelings of worth and self-esteem, our need for control, our values, belief systems, and internal messages are all part of our basic structure, as are our Type A or Type B behavioral tendencies. We all know chronic worriers, people with low self-image, and those who seem to forever choose the hardest path. Likewise, we know those who are well regarded by almost everyone, people who seem to choose their battles carefully, and many who really seem joyous in life. These are just a few facets of the kaleidoscope of personality traits that contribute to the human personality.

These traits are pieces of the stress puzzle for each of us. It is easy to see how self-esteem affects our perception of the gap between demand and ability. A high–esteem person is much more prone to see demands as positive challenges. Her internal messages reflect an "I can" attitude. The low–esteem person, however, fills her head with "I can't" messages, thereby perceiving the gap between demand and ability to be much larger.

# EXTERNAL STRESSORS

When we look outside ourselves for sources of stress, we find that they fall logically into three categories: personal, environmental, and job/career. The table below illustrates the kinds of stressors that fall into these categories.

## CATEGORIES OF STRESS

| Personal | Environmental | Job/Career |
|---|---|---|
| • Marital relationships | • Excessive noise | • Heavier than usual workload |
| • Raising children | • Smog | • Change in job duties |
| • Financial obligations | • Temperature extremes | • Lack of support from boss |
| • Deaths | • Crowding | • Lack of respect from coworkers |
| • Divorces | • Inadequate or excessive lighting | • Career change |
| • School pressures | | • Layoffs |
| • Dating pressures | | • Insufficient training |
| • In-law relationships | | • Lack of information |
| • Legal problems | | • Close deadlines |
| • Lack of support group (friends, relations) | | • Managing/ supervising others |
| • Pets | | • Lack of career options |
| | | • Insufficient pay |

This is only a partial list and it's completely generic. Take a moment to list your own current specific stressors on the following worksheet.

## MY CURRENT SPECIFIC STRESSORS

| Personal | Environmental | Job/Career |
| --- | --- | --- |
| | | |
| | | |
| | | |
| | | |
| | | |
| | | |
| | | |
| | | |
| | | |
| | | |
| | | |
| | | |
| | | |
| | | |
| | | |
| | | |
| | | |
| | | |
| | | |
| | | |
| | | |
| | | |
| | | |
| | | |

Although we can cite many different sources of stress, we would probably choose to eliminate totally only a small number of them. Some of our stressors are positive. Did you list your positive ones, too? In addition to those we acknowledge as completely positive, others have positive aspects to them. How many of your stressors are combinations (sometimes positive, sometimes negative)? Take a moment to go back and put a (+) next to those that are completely positive and a (−) next to the negative ones. Put both signs next to the combination ones. Many people find that the majority of items on their list are combination stressors.

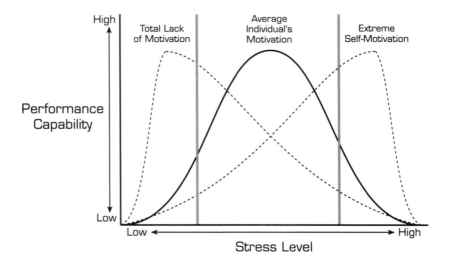

## Our Individual Differences

To a great degree, we all choose how much stress to endure in order to satisfy our desire to accumulate wealth, achieve status, and be happy in our relationships. At the far left end of the above scale are those few individuals who desire no more than adequate food, water, clothing, and shelter. They shun involvement of any kind, often living a hermit's existence, free from the stress that comes with a job, possessions, and other people. Very few people exist at this end of the scale. We're not really made for that kind of life, and those who choose it are usually mentally unstable or have been greatly damaged, emotionally, early in life.

At the far right side of the stress continuum are those individuals who are possessed by a cause or a calling. They have chosen to devote themselves totally to an ideal or a quest. This kind of complete devotion usually requires a tremendous mental capacity and a great deal of sacrifice. Some research scientists, medical professionals, and a few company CEOs approach this end of the scale. They frequently sacrifice their social life and most relationships in the process of achieving some level of greatness.

**It is impossible to predict how any single individual will respond to a particular stressor.**

It is impossible to predict how any single individual will respond to a particular stressor. Humans seek out stress-inducing situations and cover a great spectrum of stress tolerance. Nobel prize laureate Albert Szent-Gyorgyi described human activity as being "dominated by the search for happiness and fulfillment, a state in which all needs, material or intellectual, are satisfied. Pleasure is the satisfaction of a need and there can be no great pleasure without a great need. Ability brings with it the need to use that ability."

Most of us, however, fall somewhere in the middle range; some closer to the right side of the scale, some toward the left. It is important to our emotional and mental well-being that we acknowledge the choices we have made that led us to our current condition. We chose our jobs, our mates, our friends and whether or not to bear and raise children or to acquire a mortgage on a home or a loan on a car. If we are now terribly unhappy with some of those choices and the current state of our lives, we are the only ones who have the power to change them. And change them we must in order to regain our health and equilibrium.

## Lack of Control

One additional external factor worth noting has to do with control. In 1990, a research project at Cornell Medical School demonstrated that the most stressful jobs are not necessarily the riskiest or busiest (air traffic controllers, police officers, doctors), but rather those combining big demands with a relative lack of autonomy (executive secretaries, production workers). These workers suffered three times the usual incidence of high blood pressure.

A study by Northwestern National Life Insurance found that those jobs that allow very little latitude for decision making appear to be more stress producing. The employees who experience the most stress are those in jobs that have high demand and low control. That seems to extend to lifestyles as well. The more choice we believe we have, the more content and peaceful we feel.

## Change

Change is a source of great stress in most of our lives. Change almost always produces pressure on our bodies or minds, calling upon us to marshall coping resources. Both positive and negative change produce this reaction. Again, it's our perception of impact that makes the difference.

When Barb and Kevin chose to marry and merge their lives, much change occurred. They bought a new house, so both of them had to move. Barb hyphenated her last name, phone numbers changed, and, of course, the cost of the wedding and honeymoon had a large impact on their financial status. These and many other small lifestyle changes added up to a whopping amount of change in a small timeframe. The potential for a tremendous stress reaction was present for them both, but each reacted quite differently.

Barb, who had been married before and moved many times in her life, did not see these events as particularly stressful. She took time off from work to attend to the move and wedding details and, with a few minor exceptions, enjoyed the comings and goings of friends and relatives and the many planning details that needed attention. Barb saw the financial impact as a temporary aberration, one that could be remedied in a year's time. She had increased her income steadily throughout her working life, and since she and Kevin were both healthy with good jobs, she saw no reason to be concerned about money.

For Kevin, it was a different story entirely. This was his first marriage. He had owned and lived in his small condominium for twelve years and, in fact, had moved only four times in his entire life of 42 years! He, too, decided to take time off from work. However, being more of a perfectionist, Kevin tended to internalize and dwell on the many challenges of their wedding plans and their new home. Kevin's consulting business had always done well, with repeat clients and many referrals, but the new mortgage they had just incurred was more than triple what he had been paying on the condo, and he worried that they might not have the freedom to

**It's not actually the number of changes that makes the difference, but the way we perceive or experience them.**

take time off for travel and relaxation. He lost sleep, he lost weight, and his damaged knee began to hurt constantly.

This is a typical example of how the same situation can be perceived quite differently by two different people. Research into human coping mechanisms tells us that it's not actually the number of changes that makes the difference, but the way we perceive or experience them and manage their effects. Certainly, when there are many stressors present, positive or negative, the chance of feeling increased mental pressure and some physiological symptoms is high. In the next chapter you have the opportunity to assess your stress status in a variety of ways. If you are interested in measuring the number of potentially stressful occurrences in your own recent history, pay particular attention to the Life Events Stress Rating Scale in Chapter 3.

Probably the most distressful experience of change is when it involves loss. Change in the form of loss ranges from minor (lost keys, wallet) to devastating (death of a loved one). Loss takes a heavy toll on our bodies and our spirit. The more profound the loss, the more adaptation and coping energy we need.

# CHAPTER 3

## ASSESSING YOUR CURRENT LEVEL OF STRESS

"I have learned, in whatso-ever state I am, therewith to be content."

—PHILIPPIANS

You probably were motivated by more than simple curiosity when you bought this book. Today, in our fast-paced lives, it's becoming more and more common to feel greater pressure than we're comfortable having. This pressure comes from the internal and external stressors in our lives. Some of the external stressors enter our lives in the form of *events,* and these events range from fairly routine to life-changing. In 1967, Dr. Thomas Holmes and his associates demonstrated that there was a significant correlation between increases in the number and severity of life-changing events and the feelings of stress and likelihood of illness. He developed the Social Readjustment Rating Scale as a measure of this phenomenon.

The scale shown in the accompanying worksheet is based on the Social Readjustment Rating Scale by Holmes and R. H. Rahe, but it has been updated and revised to fit a more contemporary society.

# LIFE EVENTS STRESS RATING SCALE

Place a checkmark in the extreme right-hand column to indicate those events that have occurred in your life during the past twelve months.

| Life Event | Value | ✓ |
|---|---|---|
| Death of spouse | 100 | _____ |
| Death of child | 100 | _____ |
| Divorce or separation from mate | 85 | _____ |
| Arrest and incarceration in jail or other penal institution | 85 | _____ |
| Major illness or incapacitating injury | 80 | _____ |
| Marriage | 75 | _____ |
| Conviction of felony | 75 | _____ |
| Firing or layoff from job | 70 | _____ |
| Birth or adoption of new family member | 68 | _____ |
| Purchase and move to a new home | 60 | _____ |
| Foreclosure on mortgage (of residence) | 60 | _____ |
| Change in job/career | 58 | _____ |
| Giving up job to return to school | 58 | _____ |
| Change of residence (no purchase involved) | 52 | _____ |
| Major change in health of resident family member | 47 | _____ |
| Major change in lifestyle (coming out as gay/lesbian, entering religious order, joining or leaving a commune/cult) | 45 | _____ |
| Building or remodeling a home | 42 | _____ |
| Pregnancy | 40 | _____ |
| Death of close friend | 38 | _____ |
| Major change in work environment or responsibilities (new department, promotion, reorganization, different hours, new boss) | 35 | _____ |
| Major change in financial condition (inheritance, spouse takes or leaves job, significant raise) | 35 | _____ |
| Start of new romantic relationship | 33 | _____ |
| Reconciliation with spouse | 33 | _____ |
| Major change in health of in-law | 28 | _____ |
| Addition or subtraction of household member (son or daughter leaves for college, elderly parent moves in) | 27 | _____ |
| Acquiring a substantial loan | 26 | _____ |
| Beginning or ending schooling | 25 | _____ |

*(continues)*

## LIFE EVENTS STRESS RATING SCALE *(continued)*

| Life Event | Value | ✓ |
|---|---|---|
| Winning significant award (receiving college degree, publishing book or paper) | 25 | _____ |
| Changing schools | 23 | _____ |
| Minor change in physical health (increased headaches, stomach trouble, minor surgery) | 21 | _____ |
| Minor change in emotional health (mild depression, sexual difficulties, insomnia) | 19 | _____ |
| Major change in eating habits (radical diet, becoming vegetarian) | 19 | _____ |
| Election to office (public, school organization, professional society, club) | 17 | _____ |
| Change in social habits (going out a lot more/less, socializing with different people) | 16 | _____ |
| Conviction of misdemeanor or minor law violation (traffic ticket, disturbing the peace) | 15 | _____ |
| Planning and taking a vacation | 15 | _____ |
| Celebrating major holiday (Christmas, Jewish High Holy Days, Easter, Passover, Feast of Ramadan, Cinco de Mayo, Chinese New Year) | 10 | _____ |
| Acquiring new hobby, skill, sporting activity | 10 | _____ |
| (Other) | assign your own value | |
| _____ | | |
| _____ | | _____ |
| Total | | ═══════ |

Sum the values of all checked items. If an event has occurred more than once, give yourself *1.5 times* the value of the item.

**What Your Score Means:** Holmes and Rahe determined from their research that total scores of 300 or more were significantly linked to the occurrence of stress-related illness (80 percent chance). Scores of 150–299 had a 50 percent chance for occurrence of illness, and scores of 0–149 had a 30 percent chance. If your score is in the upper ranges, you are doing the right thing by investigating the sources of your stress and doing something about it. If you scored in the low range, you still may have good reason to concern yourself with stress reduction.

**The majority of our stress comes not from life-changing events but rather from everyday hassles and challenges.**

In the research for their new *Coping and Stress Profile®,* Carlson Learning Systems found that in today's fast-paced world, the majority of our stress comes not from life-changing events, but rather from everyday hassles and challenges. Child care arrangements, household errands, commuter traffic, noisy work areas, freeway jams, yard maintenance, lunch lines, bill paying, and adjustable mortgages are all merely part of everyday life for many of us.

Perhaps the most profound element in this finding is the recognition that society grants us *permission* to be emotional and act differently when major catastrophes occur. It gives us permission to grieve or miss work or take a leave of absence. More important, possibly, is that we give *ourselves* permission. This is clearly not the case with life's little irritants. However, it's just those *little* irritants that build, one upon another, unnoticed, until we get sick, rail angrily at a child or spouse, or even become violent with ourselves or others.

## EVERYDAY HASSLES AND FRUSTRATIONS

Take the time now to list the frustrations, irritants, and hassles that occur regularly in your life. In the degree column, put a capital *M* to indicate major impact and small *m* to indicate minor impact.

Hassles or Frustrations                                                    Degree

1. _____

   _____   _____

2. _____

   _____   _____

3. _____

   _____   _____

4. _____

   _____   _____

## EVERYDAY HASSLES AND FRUSTRATIONS *(continued)*

Hassles or Frustrations                                                      Degree

5. _____

   _____     _____

6. _____

   _____     _____

7. _____

   _____     _____

8. _____

   _____     _____

The other side of the stress/frustration coin is satisfaction. The Carlson research team found that a high level of stress sometimes went hand-in-hand with a low level of satisfaction in life, but not always. As mentioned earlier, it is possible to have high levels of stress *and* high levels of satisfaction, especially for people who perceive they have a lot of control over their situation. The assessment that follows is an opportunity to gauge your current level of satisfaction. Respond to each statement by making a checkmark in one of the five columns. If a question doesn't apply to you at all (e.g., you aren't currently employed or do not have a significant other), just skip it.

Once you have completed the worksheet on the following pages, you will have a good baseline measure of your current stress status. Later chapters of this book offer additional opportunities to assess your life. In the next chapter, we look at the physiological and psychological phenomenon of stress and the cycle of events that occurs when we encounter one of our stressors.

# YOUR CURRENT LEVEL OF SATISFACTION

| | Definitely True | Somewhat True | Neutral or Unsure | Mostly Untrue | Definitely Untrue |
|---|---|---|---|---|---|
| **Work/Career** | | | | | |
| The work I do is challenging. | _____ | _____ | _____ | _____ | _____ |
| I have adequate responsibility. | _____ | _____ | _____ | _____ | _____ |
| The work I do suits my ability and skills. | _____ | _____ | _____ | _____ | _____ |
| The people I work with are supportive. | _____ | _____ | _____ | _____ | _____ |
| I have reasonable authority to make decisions. | _____ | _____ | _____ | _____ | _____ |
| **Money** | | | | | |
| My job/career meets my financial needs. | _____ | _____ | _____ | _____ | _____ |
| My lifestyle is comfortable. | _____ | _____ | _____ | _____ | _____ |
| I am able to save a reasonable amount of money. | _____ | _____ | _____ | _____ | _____ |
| My spouse/partner is comfortable with our income level. | _____ | _____ | _____ | _____ | _____ |
| I am preparing adequately for retirement. | _____ | _____ | _____ | _____ | _____ |
| I am comfortable with my/our current level of spending. | _____ | _____ | _____ | _____ | _____ |

*(continues)*

# YOUR CURRENT LEVEL OF SATISFACTION *(continued)*

| | Definitely True | Somewhat True | Neutral or Unsure | Mostly Untrue | Definitely Untrue |
|---|---|---|---|---|---|

### Personal

- There is someone in my life with whom I can confide almost anything.
- I enjoy my social life.
- I have friends outside my immediate family with whom I occasionally socialize.
- My friends and I sometimes share our problems with one another.
- I have a relationship of mutual respect with my friends.
- I feel comfortable with members of the opposite sex as friends.
- I enjoy sex with my partner.
- I am satisfied with my marital status (single, married, living with someone).
- My partner frequently lets me know s/he cares.
- I feel safe disagreeing with my partner.
- My partner and I are able to talk through our differences and resolve most of them.
- My partner and I share interests and have fun together.

# YOUR CURRENT LEVEL OF SATISFACTION *(continued)*

|  | Definitely True | Somewhat True | Neutral or Unsure | Mostly Untrue | Definitely Untrue |
|---|---|---|---|---|---|
| • I feel comfortable with my body (size, shape, color). | _____ | _____ | _____ | _____ | _____ |

### Home

| | | | | | |
|---|---|---|---|---|---|
| • I enjoy spending a quiet evening at home. | _____ | _____ | _____ | _____ | _____ |
| • My home is a place where I can relax and be myself. | _____ | _____ | _____ | _____ | _____ |
| • I have a hobby I enjoy. | _____ | _____ | _____ | _____ | _____ |
| • My home is a place of serenity and beauty; it nurtures me. | _____ | _____ | _____ | _____ | _____ |
| • I take pride in my home. | _____ | _____ | _____ | _____ | _____ |

### Levity and Quality of Life

| | | | | | |
|---|---|---|---|---|---|
| • I laugh frequently. | _____ | _____ | _____ | _____ | _____ |
| • I attend movies, plays, comedy clubs fairly often. | _____ | _____ | _____ | _____ | _____ |
| • I can and do laugh at myself. | _____ | _____ | _____ | _____ | _____ |
| • Sometimes my sense of humor helps me get through difficult times. | _____ | _____ | _____ | _____ | _____ |
| • I believe I am making a valuable contribution to the world in some way. | _____ | _____ | _____ | _____ | _____ |
| • I feel needed and appreciated by those who matter to me. | _____ | _____ | _____ | _____ | _____ |
| • I have a plan for my life and I am following it. | _____ | _____ | _____ | _____ | _____ |

*(continues)*

## YOUR CURRENT LEVEL OF SATISFACTION *(continued)*

|  | Definitely True | Somewhat True | Neutral or Unsure | Mostly Untrue | Definitely Untrue |
|---|---|---|---|---|---|
| • I am usually able to focus on the positives in life, rather than the negatives. | _____ | _____ | _____ | _____ | _____ |
| • I've lived my life so that if I died tomorrow, I'd feel fulfilled. | _____ | _____ | _____ | _____ | _____ |

**What Your Score Means:** Give yourself four points for every checkmark in the *definitely true* column; give yourself three points for every checkmark in the *somewhat true* column; give yourself two points for every checkmark in the *neutral or unsure* column; give yourself one point for every checkmark in the *mostly true* column; give yourself zero points for every checkmark in the *definitely untrue* column. Then add all the points together.

*Scale:*

124+     *High* level of satisfaction.

78–123     *Medium level of satisfaction.* Some areas of your life may be more satisfying than others.

0–122     *Low level of satisfaction.* This may be a good time to take a look at ways of raising your level of happiness and harmony.

# CHAPTER 4

## OUR PHYSIOLOGICAL RESPONSES TO STRESS

### STRESS CYCLE

The body has the same exact response, physiologically, to anything that impacts its equilibrium of homeostasis. Selye studied this phenomenon and labeled it the General Adaptation Syndrome (GAS).

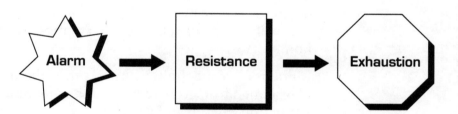

The GAS has three phases. It begins with the *alarm reaction* to an event that disrupts our normal level of functioning. This call to action generates a number of immediate physiological responses:

- Increased heart rate
- Shallow breathing
- Sweating or flushing
- Stomach spasms
- Muscle tightening

These reactions occur because the nervous system has released chemicals that give us extra strength. Fatty tissue throughout the body releases energy previously stored as fat,

**The body has the same exact response, physiologically, to anything that impacts its equilibrium or homeostasis.**

the liver releases blood sugars, and the brain commands the release of hormones that block pain.

You probably can recall a time when you experienced a strong alarm reaction. Maybe you were startled by a noise outside your bedroom window, or you watched your child take a bad tumble, or you were driving and a bicycle unexpectedly pulled out in front of you. You probably experienced some of the physiological responses mentioned above. They are all automatic biochemical reactions within the body. They exist in order to warn and prepare the body to fight, flee, or freeze in a danger situation. We share this stress reaction with other animals. If you have a dog or cat, you can observe a similar response when it sees, smells, or hears something unfamiliar.

The alarm reaction prepares us for the second stage: *resistance*. The result of the alarm reaction is that we now have an above-normal level of energy with which to resist the threat or adapt to the change and try to return to our normal state. This increase in energy is called *adaptation energy* and is usually quite effective in its attempts to bring back our homeostasis.

It doesn't last indefinitely, however. If the threat or pressure is prolonged or grows in strength, our bodies deplete that adaptation energy and the third stage, *exhaustion*, sets in. In exhaustion, some of the alarm reaction characteristics return, and this time they are irreversible. Many people today call this exhaustion stage "burnout." Studies of burnout in executives provide us with a picture of some of the warning signs for this stage:

- Sleep disturbances (inability to fall or stay asleep, disturbing and/or recurring dreams)
- Lack of enthusiasm
- Self–doubt
- Inability to make decisions

Ultimately, the final stage is a deep sense of isolation. Badly burned–out individuals have a strong feeling that no one can

**Badly burned-out individuals have a strong feeling that no one can possibly understand what's happening to them.**

possibly understand what's happening to them. Left untreated, this state of total exhaustion will almost always lead to hypertension, heart attacks, severe ulcers, and finally death.

Fortunately, most of us have coping mechanisms strong enough to mitigate that last stage. We are usually able to avoid the total burnout that leads to permanent damage. But not always. In today's world, we are seeing more and more cases of total exhaustion at all levels of the socioeconomic structure.

## THE BIG PICTURE

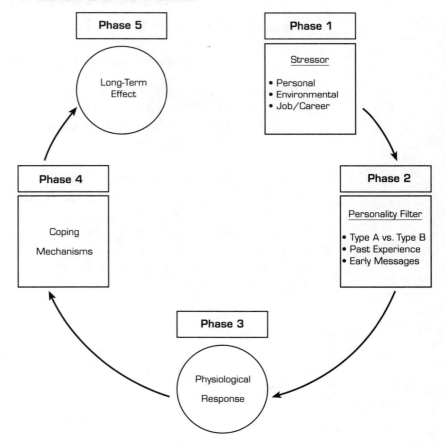

Phase 5 — Long-Term Effect

Phase 1 — Stressor
• Personal
• Environmental
• Job/Career

Phase 2 — Personality Filter
• Type A vs. Type B
• Past Experience
• Early Messages

Phase 3 — Physiological Response

Phase 4 — Coping Mechanisms

Let's put a current perspective on the clinical picture we've just painted.

**Phase 1:** We encounter one of an infinite number of internal or external stressors present in our lives today.

**Phase 2:** The stressor goes through our unique personality filter, through which we experience the situation and determine (unconsciously) whether it is indeed a "threat" to our physical, mental, or emotional being.

**Phase 3:** Our bodies (including the brain) produce a physiological response that ignites an energy boost to help us deal with the situation.

**Phase 4:** Our innate and/or learned coping mechanisms kick in, and we begin behavior designed to bring back homeostasis and peace of mind.

**Phase 5:** There may be long-term, residual effects of the incident. The event may produce emotional scar tissue, biological damage, or new improved coping mechanisms.

There are many opportunities to intervene in this cycle. In Chapter 5 we begin to take an in-depth look at Phase 3. You have the opportunity to assess your own physiological and emotional reactions to the stressors in your life. In Chapters 7 and 8, you can analyze Phase 2, your own unique personality filter, and in Chapter 9 we explore Phase 4, your coping mechanisms.

# CHAPTER 5

## SUBTLE AND NOT-SO-SUBTLE INDICATORS OF STRESS OVERLOAD

**Not only do we need some stress in our lives to survive, stress is what makes us stronger.**

As we begin to take a look at the many faces of stress, it is important to remember that stress isn't all bad. Not only do we need some stress in our lives to survive, stress is what makes us stronger. It gives us the impetus toward high performance and achievement. We use its energy to create, perform, manage, guide, produce, decide, solve, preserve, and much more. From it, we build self-confidence and pride.

Unfortunately, we are not made like the Energizer™ Bunny . . . we don't keep on going . . . and going . . . and going forever. Like a piece of machinery, overuse produces problems and eventually breakdown. We can prevent complete breakdown by understanding and recognizing the signs of stress overload.

## PHYSICAL SYMPTOMS OF STRESS

Some of the most prevalent physical symptoms are listed below. Put a checkmark next to the ones you've experienced in the past six months.

| Symptom | √ | Symptom | √ |
|---|---|---|---|
| • Heart palpitations | ____ | • Headaches (minor or migraine) | ____ |
| • Shallow or labored breathing | ____ | | |
| • Dizzy spells | ____ | • Backache | ____ |
| • Weight gain or loss | ____ | • Pains in the neck | ____ |

## PHYSICAL SYMPTOMS OF STRESS *(continued)*

| Symptom | √ | Symptom | √ |
|---|---|---|---|
| • Chest pains | _____ | • High blood pressure | _____ |
| • Constipation/diarrhea | _____ | • Increased PMS | _____ |
| • Upset stomach (indigestion, nausea, aching, vomiting) | _____ | • Eczema/psoriasis | _____ |
| | | • Accidents/clumsiness | _____ |
| • (Other) | _____ | • Impotence | _____ |
| • Increased allergic reactions | _____ | • Insomnia or constant waking | _____ |
| • Tiredness | _____ | • (Other) | _____ |
| • Nail biting | _____ | • (Other) | _____ |

## EMOTIONAL/MENTAL SYMPTOMS OF STRESS

Continue your personal assessment by marking the mental or emotional experiences you've encountered during the past six months.

| Symptom | √ | Symptom | √ |
|---|---|---|---|
| • Flagging energy | _____ | • Decrease in quantity or quality of work | _____ |
| • Craving for alcohol or drugs | _____ | • Resisting going to work | _____ |
| • Food cravings | _____ | • Feeling overwhelmed | _____ |
| • Loss of appetite | _____ | • Constant worrying/obessing | _____ |
| • Nightmares | _____ | • Feeling constantly rushed | _____ |
| • Phobias | _____ | • Feelings of isolation | _____ |
| • Anger (expressed or contained | _____ | • Forgetfulness/misplacing things | _____ |
| • Lack of sexual interest | _____ | • Emotional outbursts | _____ |
| • Feeling of anxiety | _____ | • Increased arguing/fighting with spouse, boss, colleagues | _____ |
| • Foot or finger tapping (or other nervous habits/tics) | _____ | | |
| • Excessive smoking | _____ | • Feeling victimized or powerless | _____ |
| • (Other) | _____ | • (Other) | _____ |
| • Relationship problems or dissatisfaction | _____ | | |

## STRESS-DISEASE LINK

Medical scientists are still in disagreement as to the effects of external stress (job, family, personal) on health and disease.

The work of Friedman and Rosenman linking certain behaviors (Type A) to heart disease was groundbreaking and pivotal to our current thinking, but it doesn't actually provide a direct link between high stress situations and actual incidence of disease, as many assume.

**In recent years, the intrigue and suspicion around the link between stress and health have led to a new field of medicine.**

When one digs deeply into the medical literature on *any* subject, it is not hard to find studies that either "prove" or "disprove" a particular hypothesis (e.g., stressful jobs cause increased incidence of heart attacks in males over age 55). However, in recent years the intrigue and suspicion around the link between stress and health have led to a new field of medicine: *psychoneuroimmunology.* And even though this research field has a fancy new name, the ideas have been around much longer. The Greek physician Galen noted over 2,000 years ago that depressed people were more apt to get sick. More recently, interest and popular belief were rejuvenated by books such as Norman Cousins' *Anatomy of an Illness,* in which Cousins describes his dramatic recovery from chronic illness by changing his thought patterns and affirmations.

We've known for some time that the adrenal glands take orders from the brain to release stress-combat hormones when the brain perceives a threat. Prolonged release of those same stress hormones appears to impair action of antibodies and lymphocytes, key elements in the immune defense system. Quite a number of studies now suggest that the brain communicates directly with the immune system via nerve fibers that connect to the lymph nodes, bone marrow, spleen, and other immune system components.

Scientists have observed evidence of immune system dysfunction in the incidence of illness among those involved in divorce, natural disasters, and the death or illness of a loved one. A healthy immune system is always on the prowl, seeking and destroying mutant cells, bacteria, and foreign substances. A stress-damaged system may malfunction and allow bacteria, viral infection, and cancerous cells to grow and multiply.

We simply can't draw definite conclusions about the stress-disease link, but we do know that human contact and the opportunity to share our experiences, our fears, our pain, and our triumphs are widely acknowledged to be effective stress reduction techniques. Cancer and AIDS patients are almost always encouraged to seek out support groups. In fact, the *New England Journal of Medicine,* in an update on the status of psychoneuroimmunology, reported that the use of support groups and/or counseling improved the outcome for cancer patients.

In communities all over the country, there are thousands of support groups for both psychological and medical conditions. They are there to help the families *and* the sufferers of just about any circumstance you could name. One certainly doesn't have to look very far to find countless incidents of improved medical condition as a result of the use of support groups to relieve the loneliness and isolation of a prolonged illness.

# CHAPTER 6

## CULTURAL AND SOCIETAL FACTORS: LIVING IN THE 1990s AND BEYOND

Millions of people in the United States and other industrialized nations are increasingly concerned about their mental and emotional well-being. And labor statistics show us that it is well-justified concern.

- Stress is now the leading cause of physical and emotional illness among U.S. workers.
- The National Council on Compensation Insurance reports that workplace stress is now responsible for over 13 percent of all occupational disease claims.
- In a 1991 study conducted by M. Healy, jobs were cited by 27 percent of workers as the single greatest stress factor in their lives.
- In 1988, *The Wall Street Journal* reported that 46 percent of employees indicated high levels of work-related stress and 70 percent had experienced some kind of stress-related illness.
- In 1991, *The Wall Street Journal* reported that one in six working mothers with children under age 14 maintained a night job or rotating shift.
- In Japan, a new term, *Karoshi,* was coined to mean death from overwork. The Japanese government found that 43 percent of Tokyo's salaried employees were concerned that this would happen to them.

How did this happen? Back in the late 1950s economists, sociologists, and business schools shared a great concern: too much leisure time. Productivity was increasing, automation

**Stress is now the leading cause of physical and emotional illness among U.S. workers.**

was on the rise, workers' hours had been decreasing since the turn of the century and surely would continue to do so. Pretty soon the four-day work week would become the norm, then maybe a three-day work week. What would people do with so much leisure time??

Obviously, these dire events never occurred. What actually happened was that in the mid-1960s the average work time began to climb again. A graph that had showed a steady decline for over half a century suddenly shifted. It was not limited to select occupations, either. This shift affected the greater majority of workers in the United States. With the exception of a few small blips in certain heavy industries, we entered an era of steadily increasing prosperity.

Juliet Schor, in *The Overworked American,* reminds us of the price we have paid for that prosperity. Since World War II we have seen a dramatic increase in our standard of living. The cost of that prosperity has been a much more demanding worklife. We get seduced easily by what Schor calls the "work and spend cycle" in order to keep pace with our neighbors and our own expectations of creating a more prosperous lifestyle than that of our parents.

## OUR FRANTIC LIVES

The juggling act between job and family has proved to be many an American's major source of distress in recent years. Half the population says they have too little time for family. This is particularly true for women, especially those with children. Factoring in paid and nonpaid work, Schor has calculated that the average working mother puts in a sixty-five-hour workweek. A growing number of workers are supplementing their income by taking a second job or moving very far away from the urban center. It is becoming less uncommon to find individuals who spend up to four hours a day commuting.

Sleep is another casualty of today's worklife. Sleep researchers report that the average American is getting between 60

**The average American is getting between 60 and 90 minutes per night less sleep than needed to maintain good health.**

and 90 minutes per night less sleep than needed to maintain good health. Americans are also taking less time off from work. After more than 30 years of increasing paid time away from work (vacation, sick days, holidays), the trend has reversed. Schor calculates the current shrinkage rate at 3.5 days per year; workers in 1989 spent the equivalent of four weeks more per year on the job than their counterparts in 1969.

## CHANGES IN THE STRUCTURE OF WORK

Those of us who were raised in the 1970s or earlier probably had parents with somewhat simpler lives. There were far fewer two-income households, the workday generally ended by five o'clock in the afternoon, and the wage earner (usually, but not always, the father) most likely worked for the same company his entire working life. Those days are clearly gone! Even at such large, traditional companies as Ford, IBM, AT&T, and Lockheed, at which one could once assume "lifetime employment," workers no longer have the sense that their companies are making lifetime investments in them.

In today's world, employees must take responsibility for updating their skills on a regular basis. Many companies offer nothing more in the way of training than opportunities for self-improvement and the promise that having a breadth of skills and experience will be of value in the long term. The recent trend toward downsizing and mergers, the yo-yo hiring and layoff, and the dramatic rise and fall of fortune in today's business world has dramatically decreased the job security most skilled or educated workers once relied upon for stability in their lives.

The result is today's employees assume that a game not unlike "musical chairs" is constantly taking place in their companies. To avoid being caught without a chair, we must all be flexible about the kind of assignments we accept, stay visible to upper management by taking on challenging (sometimes thankless) tasks, and continuously update our skills in an effort to keep pace with ever-changing technology.

Our current business environment is one in which companies must meet stiff competition from at home and abroad. That often means doing more with less and undergoing frequent changes. As employers reorganize, flatten hierarchical management structures, and push decision making to lower and lower levels, employees today find themselves caught in a squeeze where any show of flagging support or willingness to "do what it takes" could find them on the street.

Travel demands often add to the pressure of trying to create a well-balanced life. Even those who like a varied worklife that involves being on the road report that the hassles of airport delays, luggage mismanagement, rental car lines, time zone swapping, and hotel food eventually take their toll. In addition, those who travel frequently don't get to share the sense of community claimed by the stationary workforce.

As we try to keep our jobs, meet our lifestyle expectations, raise healthy kids, and stay financially afloat, our lives become complex to the point of collapse. Two-income families haven't figured out how to juggle jobs and family duties. Most employers won't or can't help, and employees voice frustration and anger when queried. Rather than an increase, we're seeing a decrease in time away from work. People are even going to work when they're sick, out of fear that they'll lose ground in the great race to keep their current employment. Life is no longer simple for most of us, and we feel the mounting stress in our bodies and our souls.

# PART  II

## LOOKING FORWARD

## Taking Action

First, let's consider what we know about our friend and foe: stress. We have looked at the nature and origin of stress and acknowledge that stress is inevitable in all of our lives. We need stress to live and thrive. We know that it comes from both life-shattering events and everyday challenges. Different people react differently to stressful situations; perception is the determining factor in the extent to which any one stressor affects a particular individual. Among the many vari-

**"What you can do is limited only by what you can dream."**

—DICK RUTIN,
*VOYAGER PILOT*

ables that make humans unique in this way are past experiences, personality type, and level of self-esteem.

We've explored the large role played by cultural factors in the increase of pressure we feel in today's world. The media bring to our living rooms and computer screens up-to-the-minute information and films of serial murders, royal divorces, ethnic cleansing, CEOs' salaries, animal cruelty, and celebrity courtroom drama. We live with our minds in the future far more than the here-and-now. And most of us accept without question the socially sanctioned behavior of holding in our thoughts and feelings for fear of some kind of reprisal.

Early warning signs of stress overload vary from one individual to another, and they can be both physical and emotional. It's important for all of us to monitor these indicators and take action when we see a significant increase in our own personal barometers.

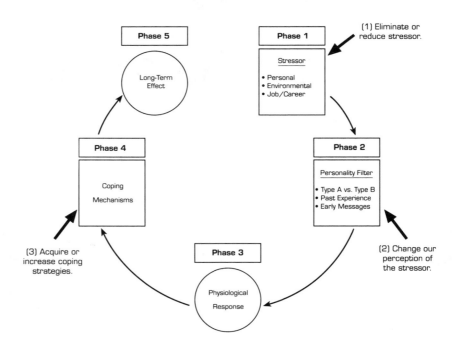

Part II of this book focuses on action. Now that we understand stress and know how to assess its whereabouts and toll, we need a personal plan for lowering the level of stress and raising the level of satisfaction in our lives. There are three ways of dealing with stress in our lives: (1) Eliminate or reduce the stressor, (2) change our perception of the stressor, or (3) acquire or increase coping strategies. These three methods differ by where they impact the stress cycle (as shown in the preceding diagram).

The next three chapters offer you opportunities to intervene at significant points in the stress cycle to lower the level of pain or discomfort that comes with stress overload and to raise your satisfaction quotient.

# CHAPTER 7

## ELIMINATING OR REDUCING THE STRESSORS

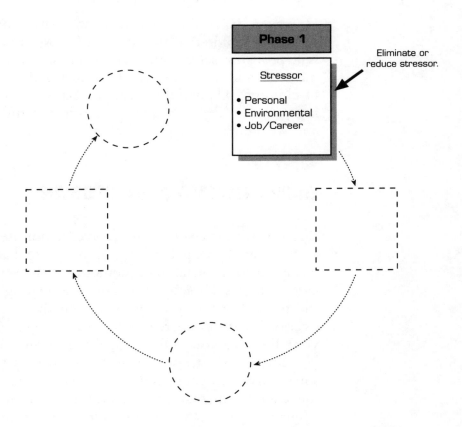

Eliminating or even reducing a stressor is the easiest, and at the same time the most difficult, approach to alleviating the pressure in our lives. After completing the exercises in the first part of this book, you should now be very aware of the source(s) of your stress. Yet how willing are you to eliminate any of your major stressors?

If you pinpointed your work—and specifically your relationship with your boss—as being the source of most of your stress, you *may,* in fact, be willing to begin the long and difficult task of finding other employment. Good for you! That's the most straightforward way of approaching this stress-management project. And if you are in a "buyers market" for employment and can pick and choose your next employer, you'll be better armed to ask questions about the environment and the demands of the job, as well as how and by whom you'll be supervised.

However, if you identified your relationship with your spouse or children as the source of most of your stress, you will probably select other approaches; divorce is a drastic measure, and we don't even have that option when it comes to children. Thankfully, there are many other ways of dealing with the stress that often comes from family interactions, and we address those ideas below.

## ELIMINATING A STRESSOR

Eliminating a stressor often involves major life changes such as moving, leaving a relationship, going back to school, changing jobs, or taking a demotion. Many people do decide to take such action, because eliminating the stressor is the most direct way of dealing with the pressure of stress overload. Let's evaluate whether or not there are stressors in your life that you could actually eliminate. In Chapter 2, you listed your stressors from three areas of your life (personal, environmental, and job/career). Using the data from the exercise in that chapter and any additional ideas that occur to you, create a list of your top ten sources of *negative* stress.

If you are not able to fill in all ten lines, it's not a problem. You probably have either less overall stress or you may have isolated the few critical sources that truly cause unpleasant situations in your life. Whatever number you have, if it feels complete to you, it's right.

## SOURCES OF NEGATIVE STRESS

1. _____
2. _____
3. _____
4. _____
5. _____

6. _____
7. _____
8. _____
9. _____
10. _____

Further analyze your list by asking yourself which of these situations you are able and willing to completely eliminate from your life. *Circle those items.* You may have several items, you may have one item, you may have zero items that you are willing to eliminate.

As we begin to formulate a plan for making a major change, however, it's important to step back and once more consider the big picture. Unless you have just recovered from a life-threatening health crisis and your doctor has told you to make drastic changes to your lifestyle immediately, don't rush into it. As part of your plan, consider including one or more of the following elements:

1. *Take a "timeout" to think it over.* Put some time and space between you and the situation. Sometimes a vacation puts things in perspective, and you may decide to take less drastic action (at least as a trial measure).
2. *Make a list.* List all the people in your life who will be affected by this action and their probable reaction.
3. *Talk to people you trust and get their input.* Ask them to be totally honest with you and really listen to what they have to say. Often, people who care about us see a very different picture than we do and can help us take into account factors we never considered. Be sure to ask for their confidentiality if necessary.
4. *Share your plans with family and friends.* Enlist their support and ask for their ideas on following through with your plan.

**Don't judge yourself by anyone else's standards or capabilities.**

One more consideration of note: We are all different. The number of assignments or tasks or obligations with which you are comfortable may vary considerably from that of your colleagues or your boss or your friends. This isn't about *their* comfort level, it's about *yours*. Don't judge yourself by anyone else's standards or capabilities. It's also unfair to judge them by yours.

Now we can proceed with the plan. For each of your circled items, fill out a Stressor Elimination Action Plan. Treat the form as a guide. Be creative with it, and by all means go beyond the simple boundaries of the form. If you need more than the two provided, copy the plan outline as many times as you need.

## STRESSOR ELIMINATION ACTION PLAN

- Stressor to be eliminated: _____
- I will eliminate this stressor on or before: ____/____/____.
- Actions I will take to eliminate it are:

1. _____
_____

2. _____
_____

3. _____
_____

4. _____
_____

5. _____
_____

## STRESSOR ELIMINATION ACTION PLAN

- Stressor to be eliminated: _____
- I will eliminate this stressor on or before: ____/____/____.

- Actions I will take to eliminate it are:

1. _____
_____

2. _____
_____

3. _____
_____

4. _____
_____

5. _____
_____

## REDUCING A STRESSOR

You may not have been able to eliminate totally any of your major stressors. That's okay. It doesn't mean you can't do some very helpful things to reduce the stressor or its impact. Let's take the major stress–source areas one at a time and consider some stressor *reduction* actions.

### Taking Charge of Your Personal Life

Many of us compound our personal lives with more activities than we can realistically juggle and continue to perform well. One strategy for limiting our commitments is to prioritize all our activities and eliminate or limit those at the bottom of the list. It is especially important at the personal level to share these strategies with friends and colleagues so that we don't cause misunderstandings or bad feelings when we become less available or less visible. Let the important people in your life know what you're doing and why. They will understand. And they will respect your ability and willingness to take charge of your life and make these changes.

If you are involved in professional societies, benevolent organizations, charity fund-raising groups, or clubs of the sort

**Many of us compound our personal lives with more activities than we can realistically juggle.**

that require attendance at meetings or performance of other duties, ask yourself how you are *really* benefiting from these memberships and what price you are paying to continue them. Yes, charitable organizations are honorable endeavors and society needs people to devote time and effort to them, but what is this commitment doing to your relationship with your children? Your spouse? Your ability to do your job? Maybe this isn't the best time in your life to pursue altruistic ventures. A plan to devote time during your retirement years or after your kids are grown might be more realistic and sensitive to everyone involved.

One way of limiting your involvement with organizations is to step down from the time-consuming leadership positions. You can still make valuable contributions even if you're not holding office. You'll also give yourself a great deal more flexibility in terms of time and effort.

Limiting and prioritizing also extend to the activities we engage in with children and spouse. If you find yourself getting caught up in the commitments of your loved ones to an uncomfortable extent, you need to cut back. Once again, this first involves communication. You must share your concern and your needs. Remember: *It's about you!* Don't make *them* wrong for your past inability to say no. Tell them what you can and cannot do. Prioritize with them. Get them involved in helping you meet your "stress overload challenge." They really do want to help you stay healthy and happy; it makes their lives better, too.

## Taking Charge of Your Job/Career

Reducing stress overload at work is similar to the approach we used with our personal life. It mainly involves analysis through prioritization. However, whether or not you are a manager (or supervisor) of others will be pivotal in your overload reduction strategy at work.

In today's work world, thousands of people, some of them only a few years out of school, are promoted and asked to manage the work of others without any prior or subsequent

**The art and science of *delegating* is one of the most important ingredients in managing effectively.**

training. Often the promotion is awarded on the basis of the fine work the individual did as a solo contributor. Management brings with it dozens of challenges, and unfortunately, few people are innately equipped to perform those functions adequately without good modeling and instruction.

The art and science of *delegating* is one of the most important ingredients in managing effectively. By far, the single greatest factor in reducing overload for managers is their willingness and ability to delegate. Many excellent workers drown in management because they hang on to such beliefs as "I can do the job faster/better than anyone else" or "I just can't trust anyone else to do it correctly" or "by the time I show her how to do it, I might as well have done it myself anyway." These sentiments are poison to management success.

If you are in management and feeling overloaded, chances are very good that you are not delegating effectively. If you don't believe that, at least go to several people you trust with whom you work closely (your subordinates are candidates for this, as well as management colleagues) and ask them to tell you honestly how they rate your ability and willingness to delegate.

Delegating is also your greatest tool in relieving your work overload. So even if you are already delegating, you may want to pump it up even more. It is a skill that can be learned like any other. Many good training programs exist for building your delegating skill. If you do not have access to these programs at your worksite, check with the human resources or training department at your company about public programs you might attend. If no training is available to you, there are also many good management primers that have whole chapters devoted to delegation. There are even a few books that address delegating exclusively. This presupposes, of course, that you are willing to put these new ideas into practice and let go of the old beliefs about how you are the only person in the universe who could possibly do the job right!

If you are not in a management position or if you are expected to perform both management tasks and some hands-on work, you will probably want to follow this next approach. It is also helpful to managers in their decision making about which tasks to delegate.

1. List all your current projects, tasks, and ongoing responsibilities.
2. Prioritize the list by arranging the items in order of importance to your organization, putting the most important at the top (number 1 on the accompanying chart).
3. Determine how many hours you spend on each task during an average week.
4. Decide how many hours you are able and willing to work each week.
5. Draw a line at the point in the list where your cumulative hourly total equals the number of hours you are willing to work.
6. Brainstorm (on your own or with a trusted colleague or friend) ways of accomplishing the tasks below the line without significant time contribution from you.
7. Share the information with your boss or team (optional).

Sharing the information with your manager or team is *optional* only if you think you can restructure your worklife based on this formula without anyone else's knowledge or input. If the tasks below the line must still be done and you need to enlist the help of others to do them, you're probably going to have to communicate your needs and decisions to your colleagues. You may want to enlist their aid in brainstorming creative ways to do more with less involvement. Beware, however; they'll probably turn around and ask you to help them do the same. You may just find ways in which you can restructure or streamline the work in your entire department so that everyone feels less stressed and the important tasks are still accomplished.

Your relationship with your manager or supervisor is usually critical to your ability to modify your worklife. Most managers are reasonable human beings with pressures and demands of their own. They are probably wrestling with many

## JOB BREAKDOWN

| Task | Hours per Week | Cumulative Hours |
|---|---|---|
| 1. | | |
| 2. | | |
| 3. | | |
| 4. | | |
| 5. | | |
| 6. | | |
| 7. | | |
| 8. | | |
| 9. | | |
| 10. | | |

Etc.

**Life changes, whether major or minor, take commitment, dedication, tenacity, and perseverance.**

of the same challenges that led you to pick up this book. If you are to make meaningful changes in your job, you will need your manager as an ally. You can probably prioritize your task list with a fair degree of certainty, but it's often extremely enlightening to get your manager's input before acting. A manager may be aware of new information that hasn't reached your ears or may simply have a different perspective on the importance of the functions you perform. If you have been unable to establish a positive relationship with your manager and see absolutely no hope of that changing, you would probably feel more comfortable planning for elimination of a stressor (job or department change) than struggling to act on the information on stressor reduction.

Life changes, whether major or minor, take commitment, dedication, tenacity, and perseverance. Changing jobs, moving to a new community, retiring, and starting life with a new partner are some of the ultimate life changes. Before undertaking drastic measures of this sort (unless they are part of a long-term prior plan), take a look at interim possibilities. For example:

- Try part-time work.
- Take time off.
- Move to a smaller house (smaller mortgage).
- Ask grown children to establish residency outside of your home.
- Try *teaching* instead of *doing*.
- Take a demotion.
- Resign from volunteer work.
- Go to counseling (with or without your spouse).

These are examples of a few creative ways others have found to ease the pressure of "life in the fast lane." You can probably come up with lots more that are worth trying before you make that major life change, especially if major change involves cutting yourself off from positive aspects of life as well as negative. However, change might be the most positive move you could make, and if in the final analysis you decide to go for it, put your heart and soul into it and don't let anyone tell you otherwise!

# CHAPTER 8

## CHANGING OUR PERCEPTION

Our second opportunity for intervening in the stress cycle is in how we perceive the stressor. Remember Barb and Kevin's wedding from Chapter 2? Both of them faced the same actual stressors (home purchase, moving, wedding planning, visiting relatives), but because of their unique past histories, they responded to the events very differently. In other words, their *perceptions* of the events differed.

Changing our perception can sound incredibly simple, and a few people profess to being able to change their own per-

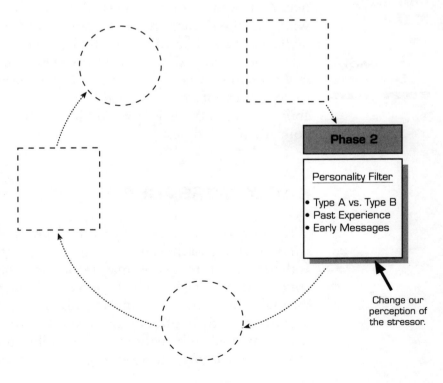

Phase 2

Personality Filter

• Type A vs. Type B
• Past Experience
• Early Messages

Change our
perception of
the stressor.

ception whenever they choose, simply by deciding to do it. If it were in fact easy, all any of us would ever have to do would be to say to ourselves "the effect this situation is having on me is undesirable; from now on I will see it differently," thereby eliminating any potential for stress. Henceforth, whenever your boss called you into his office for a little chat about that failed project, you would be able to approach it eagerly, knowing it would lead only to greater knowledge for you and an enhanced ability to use what you had learned to achieve success in the future. And when your teenager arrived home at 2 A.M., stinking of beer, handed you the car keys, and announced that your car was making a funny new noise, you'd be able to have a good laugh with her, tell her about your first taste of beer, and agree to go for a little drive tomorrow to listen to the car's new noise, after which you'd fall into a sound, blissful sleep.

> **"Nothing is good or bad, but thinking makes it so."**
>
> —**WILLIAM SHAKESPEARE**

Does any of this sound familiar to you? I doubt it. Most people find that changing their perception to a stressor, though simple in theory, is extremely difficult to do in practice. As I'm sure you've observed, however, individuals vary wildly in their reactions to stressors, and it is possible, with dedication and commitment, to begin to change some of our unproductive thought patterns. This is especially necessary for those of you who find that your fears and reactions to certain events are so stressful that they are crippling your ability to function as you would like in the world, or enjoy your life to the fullest.

## EARLY MESSAGES

Why do people react so differently from one another to the same exact situation? There are several intertwined reasons, and the common denominator for most of them is early childhood messages, which serve to program our lives through our unconscious minds, like indelible tape recordings that play throughout our lives. Like it or not, the verbal and nonverbal information your childhood care-givers (in most cases parents and teachers) imparted to you took on profound importance in the formation of your own reactions to subsequent events. Understanding this phenomenon and analyzing your own early messages become the first step toward unraveling the puzzle of your current reactions to stressful situations.

**Under-standing alone won't change anything.**

Understanding alone won't change anything. Let's compare our unconscious mind with a dark attic. Most people stumble around reacting to events and situations without ever understanding why they do what they do, much as we would stumble over old furniture trying to navigate our way through a dark attic. If we switch on the light in the attic, we can now avoid the obstacles as we walk through, but the mere act of switching on the light doesn't remove the furniture; that takes a lot more time and effort. In the same way, understanding from whom those early messages came, their contents, and the way they were delivered gives us tremendous insight but very little change in our behavior or thought patterns.

More important than the subject matter of those early messages is the *paradigm* from which they were issued. A "paradigm" as it's used here is a model, pattern, or theme through which messages emanate. It might also be called a *mind set*. Some early messages come from a paradigm of *choice,* others from a paradigm of *victim.*

Messages from *choice:*

"Your father is a self-made man."
"You can play the piano if you want to."
"We moved to this house because we liked the neighborhood."
"I'm going to the store now."
"Let's eat home tonight so we can save money for the movies on Friday."
"We're having tuna casserole for dinner."
"Would you like some spinach?"
"I like it when you clean your room."
"God gave you the ability to be anything you want when you grow up."
"Dad's a plumber."

Messages from *victim:*

"Dad had to help his father when he was growing
   up."
"No one in this family could ever be musically in-
   clined."
"This neighborhood was all we could afford."
"I have to go shopping now or we'll have nothing
   for dinner."
"We can't afford to eat out tonight."
"We have to have tuna casserole tonight; we have
   no other meat."
"If you don't eat the spinach, your teeth will fall
   out."
"I can't tolerate a dirty room."
"You must choose a career and study for it."
"Everyone in this family must go to college."
"You should be a doctor like your father."
"The only work your father can do is plumbing."

As harmless as some of these "victim" messages sound, they
convey a subtle message of "we have little *choice* in life." We
must take whatever God or fate or circumstance created for
us. The *choice* messages, in contrast, communicate the
human ability to impact circumstances or events, to change
things for ourselves, to take control of our lives. Being "in
choice" is a much more powerful way to live. Some of us
grew up that way, others did not. Listen to those around
you. You'll hear it in their voices. Someone whose language
is full of such extremes as "can't," "has to," "stuck," "help-
less," "trapped," "must" is not living in choice. Such people
are living lives filled with victimization. They may be vic-
timized by a boss, a spouse, a child, a parent, a company, a
career, a custom, a law, a standard, or countless other elements against which they see themselves as powerless.

So, what's your position in all this? Here's the test: How
effectively were you able to do the exercises in Chapter 7?
Have you made a plan to eliminate or reduce some of your
stressors? If so, you're most likely living *in choice* already, and
you may want to take a look at some possibilities for shifting

your perspective or modifying your perceptions as well. If, however, rather than doing the exercises, you told yourself all the reasons why the exercises wouldn't work for you or didn't apply to you or you found ways in which you were trapped and had no choice, you may have some life-limiting *victim* messages going on in your unconscious.

We can reprogram our unconscious minds, erase the old tapes, and record new ones. It will take time, and it will take perseverance. And it can be done. During my own child-hood, I received a mixture of messages (as many of us do). Some, however, were pretty limiting. From an early age I was warned to "be careful." Much of what looked intri-guing to a five-year old seemed quite dangerous to my mother and father, including sports. Having been reasonably unathletic themselves, the early messages my parents gave me about my agility and physical abilities were not too posi-tive. They amounted to pronouncements about my lack of strength and stamina, poor coordination and balance, and the danger that flying balls presented to my head and eyes. I bought these ideas, totally, and stayed away from sports throughout my formative years.

**We can re-program our uncon-scious minds, erase the old tapes, and record new ones.**

Once in college, however, the temptation, and pressure, to try some new physical endeavors was very powerful. I tim-idly began to experiment with the activities my friends so obviously enjoyed, and although it took me much longer than most to conquer my fears and overcome those tapes in my head about poor coordination and such, I eventually became a very good skier. I also jog long distances and play tennis. But what finally transformed me from someone who occasionally dallied at a low level with these activities to an *athlete,* a true skier, a marathon runner, a tennis player was my determination to change the messages. I now *think* of myself as a person with very good balance, excellent eye-hand coordination, and an athletic body. That was the big change.

Fortunately, other messages from my parents were much more positive and allowed me a great deal more freedom and choice. As a result of being told I was smart and encouraged to explore different interests, I have always believed I could do almost anything I chose that involved powers of thinking and organizing. That allowed me to be far less stressed over college exams, new work projects, and career changes than many of my friends and colleagues. However, I still struggle right along with the countless millions who believe the only "right" choice (read "nonchoice") about body shape is *thin*.

For many of us the tapes or messages are mixed—some are positive, some are negative; some are victim messages, some are in choice. Before you can begin to reinvent your own undesirable messages, you must make an assessment of what the current tapes are playing. Use the following worksheet to survey what is going on in your unconscious.

## MY OLD TAPES

In this exercise, first list any messages/tapes you are aware of that focus on the issues noted. Then indicate ways in which these old messages lead to stressful situations.

### Personal Messages

- House cleanliness

    *Message:* _____

    _____

    *Causes me stress by:* _____

    _____


- Education (going to college, getting good grades)

    *Message:* _____

    _____

    *Causes me stress by:* _____

    _____

- Mothers who work outside the home vs. mothers who stay home
  with children

    *Message:* _____

    _____

    *Causes me stress by:* _____

    _____

- Body shape/size/weight

    *Message:* _____

    _____

    *Causes me stress by:* _____

    _____

- Athletic competition

    *Message:* _____

    _____

    *Causes me stress by:* _____

    _____

- Sharing thoughts and/or feelings with spouse

    *Message:* _____

    _____

    *Causes me stress by:* _____

    _____

- Saving money and/or accruing debt

    *Message:* _____

    _____

    *Causes me stress by:* _____

    _____

- "Expect the worst" vs. "nothing happens that you can't handle"

    *Message:* _____

    _____

*Causes me stress by:* _____

_____

- "You create your destiny" vs. "destiny is preordained by a greater force"

    *Message:* _____

    _____

    *Causes me stress by:* _____

    _____

- Other

    *Message:* _____

    _____

    *Causes me stress by:* _____

    _____

- Other

    *Message:* _____

    _____

    *Causes me stress by:* _____

    _____

## Job/Career Messages

- Professional competition

    *Message:* _____

    _____

    *Causes me stress by:* _____

    _____

- Speaking your mind to someone in authority

    *Message:* _____

    _____

    *Causes me stress by:* _____

    _____

- Handling multiple tasks

  *Message:* _____

  _____

  *Causes me stress by:* _____

  _____

- Changing jobs

  *Message:* _____

  _____

  *Causes me stress by:* _____

  _____

- Appropriate vs. inappropriate professions

  *Message:* _____

  _____

  *Causes me stress by:* _____

  _____

- Saying no to an assignment

  *Message:* _____

  _____

  *Causes me stress by:* _____

  _____

- Other

  *Message:* _____

  _____

  *Causes me stress by:* _____

  _____

- Other

  *Message:* _____

  _____

*Causes me stress by:* _____

_____

## Environmental Messages

- Quiet vs. commotion

    *Message:* _____

    _____

    *Causes me stress by:* _____

    _____

- Country vs. suburban vs. inner-city living

    *Message:* _____

    _____

    *Causes me stress by:* _____

    _____

- Other

    *Message:* _____

    _____

    *Causes me stress by:* _____

    _____

These early messages cause stress in our lives in quite a variety of ways. The more ironclad the message, the more rigid we are in our demands to have things a certain way in our lives. If you have ever been accused of being rigid, take a look at what led to your iron-bound belief in that area. Where we don't have strong messages, we tend to take a more flexible approach. Perfectionists have very strong messages about the way things should be. What do you think we would find if we compared the early messages of people with Type A personalities with those of Type B? Type B people are almost always more flexible in their outlook and demeanor.

# CHANGING THE MESSAGES

Living more of life *in choice* may mean replacing some of those early messages with new messages that are more flexible, that leave us with more options. We can do that by deliberately changing our *self-talk*. Self-talk is the way we apply those tapes to everyday situations. Since the old tapes can't actually be completely destroyed or exorcised, we need to disable them by deliberately creating new self-talk. When I did that with my athletic messages, I had to disable the old messages by replacing self-talk that sounded like "don't try that hill, it's too steep and you might fall and really hurt yourself," "going fast is unsafe, I will lose my balance and fall," "the tennis ball might poke my eye out, I better get out of the way, I'll never hit it anyway" with self-talk that produced more confidence: "I am coordinated, I'll fly down this hill like an Olympian," "I'm just like Chris Evert and I connect effortlessly with the ball," "I love being active, my body is a finely tuned machine." These kinds of statements are *affirmations*.

**Self-talk is really self-thought.**

Do these sound a little silly? In fact, our disabling self-talk sounds just as silly. But the good news is you don't have to tell anyone your self-talk, because you don't express it aloud. Self-talk is really self-*thought*. We *think* these words, but most people don't actually verbalize them. The best news is that it works. In worksheet on the following page, you have an opportunity to choose some issues on which you would like to alter your self-talk. But first, look at the following examples of affirmative self-talk.

## Examples of Affirmative Self-Talk

| Issue | Self-Talk (Affirmation) |
| --- | --- |
| • Body size | "My body is beautiful; I respect it and take good care of it." |
| | "I feed myself healthy, low-fat foods." |
| | "My body is getting healthier every day." |

| Issue | Self-Talk (Affirmation) |
|---|---|
| • New project | "I am intelligent and creative." |
| | "I am a good problem solver and I'll do an excellent job with this project." |
| | "My boss chose me for this project because I am the most qualified and will do the best job; she has faith in me, and I do too." |

Notice in the first example that I use present rather than future tense. That is because I want to stay focused in the present, not the future. I want to affirm what I am doing right now. The future is always a few days, a few weeks, a few moments away. If you use future tense ("I will feed my body healthy foods") you are making a *plan* rather than an affirmation. It's less effective.

Choose three to five issues for which you would like to create and practice new self-talk. List the issue and then design one or more positive statements about how you will approach the issue in the future. Be as specific as possible in your statements and tie them to the stress-producing messages in the last exercise.

## CREATING NEW SELF-TALK

| Issue | Self-Talk (Affirmation) |
|---|---|
| _____ | 1. _____ |
| | _____ |
| | 2. _____ |
| | _____ |
| | 3. _____ |
| | _____ |

| Issue | Self-Talk (Affirmation) |
|-------|-------------------------|
| _____ | 1. _____ |
|  | _____ |
|  | 2. _____ |
|  | _____ |
|  | 3. _____ |
|  | _____ |
| _____ | 1. _____ |
|  | _____ |
|  | 2. _____ |
|  | _____ |
|  | 3. _____ |
|  | _____ |
| _____ | 1. _____ |
|  | _____ |
|  | 2. _____ |
|  | _____ |
|  | 3. _____ |
|  | _____ |
| _____ | 1. _____ |
|  | _____ |
|  | 2. _____ |
|  | _____ |
|  | 3. _____ |
|  | _____ |

Like any new skill or activity, this new self-talk must be practiced. However, you needn't wait until the issue actually presents itself to practice the affirmations for your new be-

**At first you may not notice the slow, subtle changes in your behavior, but you'll notice people reacting differently toward you.**

havior. You can practice them any time and anywhere. Many people are successful using a schedule for practicing affirmations. One way of scheduling them is to do them at the same time each day, such as immediately after arising, right after lunch, and just before bed. The sleep researchers tell us that doing this just before sleep is particularly effective because it is the last conscious thing our minds do and therefore acts to shape our unconscious dream activity as well.

The more we practice this new self-talk, the more natural it will feel and the better able we'll be to do it when it really counts. You may want to start with affirmations for only one or two issues so that you can really give each one a lot of time and attention and notice the changes when they occur. You can move on to include others when you've had some success with the technique.

Changing your perceptions through modification in self-talk is highly effective in the long run in changing your entire demeanor from one of negativity and pessimism to that of optimism and joy. At first you may not notice the slow, subtle changes in your behavior as they happen, but I believe you'll notice people reacting differently toward you, especially new friends and colleagues. And in the years to come, you'll be quite able to look back and see the evolution from the old you to the new, more flexible, more satisfied you.

# CHAPTER 9

## ADDING AND INCREASING COPING MECHANISMS

Coping mechanisms are thought patterns and behavioral habits that neutralize stressors or mitigate their impact on us. Coping helps us manage our emotions and reactions to stressful situations. We all have many built-in coping mechanisms that kick in automatically when we need them, such as drinking more liquids when it's hot, or blocking our memory of physical pain. And we all have varying levels of learned coping techniques. Maybe you listen to soothing music during your commute or wear ear plugs to bed to

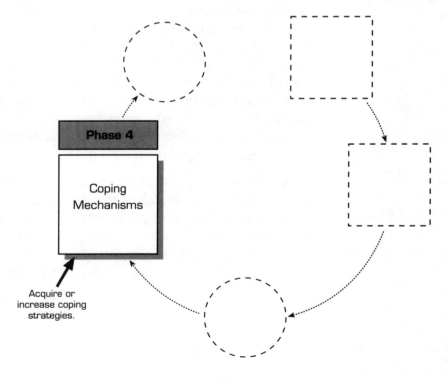

Phase 4

Coping Mechanisms

Acquire or increase coping strategies.

**We human beings have lots of options available to us.**

block out the neighbor's barking dog. These are adapted behaviors that help you deal with stressful situations. The third possibility for lowering the stress in our lives is to intervene at this level.

Intervening at the coping level generally presupposes a decision that it is not appropriate or reasonable to eliminate or reduce the stressor or to change your paradigm, hence your reaction, to the stressor. Fortunately, we human beings have lots of options available to us with regard to taking control of our lives, and there are many possibilities for increasing the coping mechanisms we already have and for developing and nurturing entirely new ones. In this chapter we look at several categories of coping strategies and explore a variety of ideas within each.

## UNHEALTHY COPING MECHANISMS

First, let's acknowledge that there are some very popular coping mechanisms that are not so healthy. Most of these come under the umbrella of *avoidance* strategies. Probably the most prevalent of these is alcohol. Admittedly, alcohol has properties that help us relax and sometimes forget (for a short period of time) our current troubles. But, like all other avoidance mechanisms, it offers only temporary help and has the likely effect of making things worse in the long run, not to mention the added problems that accompany dependency if it's carried to extremes.

Prescription drugs, nicotine, and even caffeine are part of this category of *unhealthy* coping mechanisms, not because they are illegal or even because they alter our senses or ability to function. It is because they don't really help us cope. They actually create more problems than they solve. Avoidance strategies do only one thing: postpone stress.

## EVALUATING AVOIDANCE STRATEGIES

In the following exercise, evaluate how much you depend on these and other avoidance strategies to deal with the stress in your life.

| Avoidance Strategy | Never | Sometimes | Often |
|---|---|---|---|
| • Alcohol | _____ | _____ | _____ |
| • Narcotics | _____ | _____ | _____ |
| • Other prescription drugs | _____ | _____ | _____ |
| • Nicotine (cigarettes) | _____ | _____ | _____ |
| • Caffeine (coffee, colas, chocolate) | _____ | _____ | _____ |
| • Sweet and fatty foods | _____ | _____ | _____ |
| • Refusing to communicate about the stressor (to spouse, child, boss, etc.) | _____ | _____ | _____ |
| • Frequent geographical moves | _____ | _____ | _____ |
| • Frequent job changes | _____ | _____ | _____ |
| • Frequent spouse changes | _____ | _____ | _____ |

If you marked even one of these in the "often" column, or several of them in the "sometimes" column, I encourage you to consider making the effort to replace this behavior with healthier coping techniques.

## CALMING THE BODY

Our bodies respond to stressful situations in a variety of ways, as noted in Chapter 4. Many of the physiological changes that occur within us are undesirable, unhealthy, and even dangerous if prolonged. Insomnia, fatigue, back pain, muscle stiffness, headaches, ulcers, colitis, gastritis, heart disease, cancer, and strokes have all been associated with stress and can all have debilitating effects on our bodies. In order to counteract this negative physiological impact, we must learn to reverse it. Learning to relax provides life-long control over our most vital functions.

Relaxation techniques were designed for just this purpose and have been around as long as humankind has had a written record. In addition, most of us are unable to take the time off necessary to truly unwind, so we must learn to calm our bodies more often and in quicker ways.

When you relax, your heart beat slows, your blood pressure is immediately lowered, muscle tension decreases, your body demands less oxygen, the flow of blood to your muscles and organs decreases, and your natural output of cortisone is reduced. This produces an immediate difference in the way you feel; a dramatic increase in your sense of well-being. Relaxation can be learned and doesn't require any special equipment. In fact, it doesn't even require a special location. Many people have reported significant positive changes as a result of practicing as little as two 15-minute relaxation exercises per day, each and every day.

**Relaxation can be learned and doesn't require any special equipment.**

Methods for releasing tension from our bodies are many and varied, with new ones being developed every year. Probably the most commonly known is massage, in all of its many forms. Because it involves two people, we explore massage a little later in this chapter, under the heading of "getting help." In this section we focus strictly on ways of relaxing the body that don't involve anyone but you.

## Breathing

Getting the energy we require involves not only eating nutritious foods, but ensuring adequate oxygen intake as well. Oxygen enables our digestive systems to break down the nutrients in the foods we eat so that they are accessible to us. Through our breath, we rid our body of toxins and carbon dioxide. Without this function, our cells become contaminated and we die. Most people use less than 60 percent of their breathing potential, which means that we are underutilizing the ability to expel these poisons and absorb oxygen for the blood supply, the organs, the skin, and the brain. Correct breathing is vital to our thought processes, our vitality, and our looks.

What is much more readily apparent than the effects noted above is the link between breathing and emotion. When we get excited, our breathing becomes shallow and rapid. This adversely affects our thinking. That's why common wisdom has it that "taking a few deep breaths" or "breathing deeply and counting to ten" will help us see the situation more clearly and react more effectively.

---

## A BREATHING EXERCISE YOU CAN DO ANYWHERE

Stand with your feet about hip-width apart, your knees soft (not locked) and your hands at the base of your rib cage. Slowly breathe in through your nose, without raising your shoulders. Feel your rib cage expand. Hold the breath in for a count of five, then slowly exhale through your mouth, making sure to expel all the accumulated air. Repeat this five to ten times. Notice any mental or physical changes that occur.

---

This next exercise is similar but a little more limited in its application, since it involves lying down. In this one you experience the difference between breathing with your upper body and breathing with your full diaphragm:

---

## A BREATHING EXERCISE TO DO LYING DOWN

Lie on a firm surface (a carpeted floor is excellent). Place your hands on your rib cage, with your fingers just touching. Close your eyes, breathe normally, and focus on the movement of your body beneath your hands (about 30 seconds). Now breathe in through your nose, using your full diaphragm—breathe into your chest and your abdomen. Your fingers should be forced apart. Notice how much more oxygen you are absorbing. Keep your shoulders still. Exhale thoroughly through your mouth and nose. Continue breathing in this manner for five to ten minutes, making sure your fingers are forced apart with every breath.

You will achieve the best results by practicing these exercises (either one or both) twice a day for several weeks. You will also find it beneficial to practice these for a while before moving on to the muscle relaxation exercises, because full, controlled breathing makes muscle relaxation much more effective.

## Muscle Relaxation

The exercises in this section are designed to help you get in touch with the areas in your body where you hold tension and learn to release it. You may not find them easy at first or you may feel as though you are doing them incorrectly. Do them the best you can and persevere. You'll find they will get easier for you and you'll feel less awkward after a week or so. You may also find your mind wandering during the exercises. Don't be discouraged; this is normal. Again, the more you practice, the more disciplined and focused you'll become.

You may find it helpful to have someone read the exercise to you until you have memorized its sequence. Another option is to record it yourself on audiotape and play it back whenever you want to practice. Be sure to speak very slowly as you record, and pause appropriately for each muscle activity. In addition to the exercises here, you will also find many good-quality, prerecorded relaxation tapes in your local bookstores.

## PROGRESSIVE RELAXATION EXERCISE

1. Lie on a firm surface with your arms at your sides or sit comfortably on a chair with your feet flat on the floor and your hands resting on

your knees or thighs. Close your eyes and breathe deeply several times.

2.  First tense the muscles in your feet and hold the tension for 10 seconds, then quickly release.

3.  Now do the same with your ankles, then your calves, your knees, your thighs, your buttocks, your pelvis, your abdomen, and your chest.

4.  Then begin with your fingers, moving to your hands, your wrists, your forearms, your elbows, your upper arms, your shoulders, your neck, your head, and finally your face.

5.  Now tighten all of your muscles at once, making your entire body rigid and tense. Be aware of the tightening in your jaw; bring your shoulders up to your ears; clench your teeth, pinch your face, scrunch up your fingers and toes, frown—then release all the tension at once. Let your shoulders slump, your jaw hang loose, your arms flop to the side.

6.  Repeat the full-body tension and release two more times.

7.  End by taking five full breaths, breathing slowly into the abdomen through your nose and out through your mouth. Make sure you are holding no tension anywhere in your body.

This last exercise should take approximately fifteen minutes. If you are completing it in much less time, you are doing it too fast. The value in these exercises comes from doing them very slowly, so resist the temptation to rush.

Here is another muscle relaxation exercise, one that you can do at work.

## MID-DAY WORK SURVIVAL BREAK

1.  Sit on a straight-back chair with your feet flat on the floor and your hands resting lightly on

your legs. This is your base position. You may proceed with your eyes open or closed.

2. Take three full, slow deep breaths, breathing in through your nose and exhaling through your mouth.

3. Slowly incline your head forward until your chin is against your chest or as close as you can comfortably go. Return to base position and repeat three times. Breathe deeply.

4. Tilt your head backward as far as it will comfortably go, return to base position, and repeat three times. Then tilt to the right three times, then the left three times. Remember: Breathe deeply.

5. Slowly circle your head clockwise three times, then counterclockwise three times. Breathe deeply.

6. Now bring your shoulders up toward your ears, hold for five seconds, and release. Repeat three times. Breathe deeply.

7. With the thumb and fingers of one hand, slowly massage the fleshy part of the other hand and fingers. Switch hands. Breathe deeply.

8. With your elbows on your desktop, your eyes closed, and the fleshy part of your hand below the thumb against your cheekbones, massage your brow and forehead with your fingertips. Then do the same to your temples. Breathe deeply.

## Stretching

This is really a variation on muscle relaxation that elongates and stretches the muscle rather than contracting and releasing it. The following is a basic yoga technique that is designed to increase your awareness and give you more energy by stretching your body.

## A BASIC YOGA STRETCHING TECHNIQUE

1. Stand tall with your hands at your sides. Make sure your knees are soft and your hands are relaxed. As you breathe in, turn your hands so that your palms face upward. Continue to inhale while raising your arms slowly over your head, bringing your palms together at the top of the arc above your head.
2. Keeping your arms in that position, exhale slowly as you rise up onto your toes.
3. Hold the position, breathe in, and hold your breath as you count to five.
4. As you slowly exhale, return to your starting position, gradually bringing your arms and your heels back down.
5. Take another deep breath, open your eyes, and resume work.

## Visualization

Creative visualization takes you on a mental excursion, far from the stressors of daily life. Since it is both a mind and body coping mechanism, it is best to use a tape of the following exercise or a similar one made commercially. Like relaxation, there are many wonderful guided visualizations you can purchase. Here is a visualization exercise you can tape and practice any time you need a little break and can find a quiet place to hide. Read very slowly, pausing for as much as a minute after each instruction. Your completed recording should take fifteen to twenty minutes.

## A VISUALIZATION EXERCISE

1. Close your eyes and take several slow, full deep breaths. Clear your mind of the minutiae

and begin to picture a lovely place. It could be a beach at sunset, the top of a snow-covered mountain, a lush, green meadow—anyplace that makes you feel calm, relaxed, and peaceful.

2.  Notice the details . . . what color is the sky? . . . what do you smell? . . . what is immediately underneath your feet? . . . what is the temperature like?

3.  Remember to continue to breathe deeply.

4.  Notice whether or not you're alone. Is there anyone or anything there with you in this very peaceful place? If so, ask yourself if you want him/her/it there. If you don't, gently say good-bye and make the image vanish.

5.  Now begin to explore your personal place of peace and beauty. Walk around and experience all the qualities of this place. Pick a flower . . . lie down in your meadow . . . pick up a handful of soft, fluffy snow and blow it from your hand . . . do whatever feels right in your place. Have fun in your special place.

6.  Now experience yourself as very light and buoyant. Begin to run. You cannot trip and fall because whenever you encounter an obstacle, you simply glide over it or around it or even through it. You're almost flying . . . feel the wind in your hair . . . go faster . . . now go slower, and slower, and finally come to a light, effortless landing.

7.  Notice where you are now. Maybe you're back in your special place. Maybe you are in a new and special place. Notice what's around you. Breathe deeply and absorb it into your soul.

8.  Now look far away into the horizon. Someone is coming. You recognize her/him. It's someone very special . . . it's someone you enjoy very much. Watch him/her getting closer . . . and closer . . . and closer. As s/he gets close

enough to touch, give him/her a hug or shake his/her hand or touch his/her shoulder and smile.

9. Show your special person around your special place and experience his/her enjoyment as well.

10. Now share with your special person what it is that makes him/her so special. Watch him/her smile. Now listen as your special person tells you why you are so special. Listen . . . listen . . . listen. Breathe deeply.

11. Spend as long as you like in your special place with your special person. . . .

12. Then tell him/her good-bye . . . you'll see him/her again soon. Watch him/her drift away just as he/she arrived while you focus on the joy of your friendship and love.

13. Now it's your turn to leave your special place. Leaving isn't sad . . . you can return whenever you like. Watch your special place begin to slowly lose color, fade away, and finally disappear completely.

14. When you are ready, slowly open your eyes, take a few deep breaths, and return to the present.

If you find that you enjoy this particular method for calming your body and relieving your mind, you may want to have two or three visualization tapes on hand for variety. There are hundreds of commercial ones to choose from. Some stores will let you listen to a demo so that you will know whether it is appealing before you make your purchase. You may even find that you prefer a visualization of your own creation. If it sounds like something you want to try, first compose it, then read it into a tape recorder (or have a friend read it for you). As long as it is calming to you, there are no limits to what you can create.

## Sleep

Sleep is necessary for life. It is a naturally occurring phenomenon that serves to heal the mind and body and rejuvenate the resources needed for normal daily functioning. For most of us, sleep is the easiest and most natural form of relaxation around. To an insomniac, however, sleep can seem like the holy grail. The National Sleep Institute found that over 35 percent of workers and 55 percent of managers report problems falling or staying asleep. Unfortunately, stress and insomnia seem to be bosom buddies.

**Stress and insomnia seem to be bosom buddies.**

No single theory on the amount of sleep our bodies actually need has ever gained complete acceptance among the experts. Most agree, however, that sleep deprivation is epidemic in Western society, especially since high-quality sleep (deep, uninterrupted, and untroubled) is elusive for many. Some sleep researchers go so far as to say that if you have to set an alarm to wake up, you are suffering some degree of sleep deprivation. If this is in fact the case, we are starting every day with depleted resources for coping. No wonder we experience so many minor everyday hassles as stressors!

So how can we take better advantage of sleep, our potential ally? First, we must determine how much sleep our bodies need. This differs substantially from one individual to another. We'd all be thrilled to say we could function perfectly on five hours per night, but in reality, only a tiny percentage of the population is truly able to do that. You must be totally honest in your assessment of your sleep needs.

If you are unsure just what your actual needs are, go to sleep at a "reasonable hour" (9 P.M.–11 P.M.), do not set an alarm, and see how long you sleep. The tricky part of this is that in order to get a true reading, you will need to do it continuously for at least two weeks. The problem with gauging it by how long you sleep on weekends is that most of us are sleeping longer than normal in an attempt to make up for a week-long deficit.

Once you know how much sleep you need, make a conscious effort to get that much whenever you can. A good goal is four to five times per week. This may mean that you will have to start going to bed earlier. Another possible option is to adjust your work hours so you can sleep a little longer. A thirty-something colleague of mine took a four-month sabbatical a couple of years ago and was so struck by how much better she felt and functioned when she was able to get her required 8.5 hours of sleep per night that when she returned to work, she put herself and her entire staff on a flexible schedule where each one of them could choose their own arrival time and flex the rest of their hours to meet at least an eight-hour day. She tells me it's been very successful and other managers in her firm are now trying it.

Insomnia (inability to fall asleep or stay asleep), although not truly life-threatening, is not a trivial matter to the millions who suffer from it. However, a great deal of the problem is one of mental compounding, much like sexual impotence. Let's look at an example. Elaine goes to bed late one night after staying up until 2 A.M. preparing for an important customer meeting the next day. Although she's tired and needs all the sleep she can still get, she lies there the rest of the night, tossing fretfully, unable to clear her mind of all the preparatory chatter. The next night she is exhausted and goes to bed early, but when she is not immediately able to fall asleep, she begins to worry: "I've just got to get some sleep tonight; I barely made it through today." But another night goes by with little to no sleep. The third night the same thing occurs. Now Elaine is really getting worried and begins to think she has a serious problem, labels it *insomnia,* and on it goes.

## Breaking the Cycle of Insomnia

Does Elaine have a *problem*? Yes—a mental one. Like most "insomniacs," Elaine will need to shift her *thinking* in order to break the cycle. Here are some ways of doing that.

1. Remember, insomnia is not a disease, it's a *thinking* disorder more than a *sleep* disorder.
2. Change your bedtime routine. If you are accus-

tomed to watching the news before retiring, try listening to soothing music instead. If you like to read, pick up something less stimulating and thought-provoking. Reading your own affirmations (see Chapter 8) can be very soothing.

3. Avoid stimulants. Coffee, tea, or other caffeine-laced beverages at dinner or in the evening may have agreed with you once, but our bodies change. Try herbal tea or skim milk. At least switch to a decaffeinated beverage (but remember, even "decaffeinated" drinks still have some caffeine in them).

4. Take a warm (not hot) bath. Warm water relaxes our muscles, thereby helping us calm our bodies.

5. Exercise every day. Nothing aids sleep like *physical* exhaustion (totally different from mental exhaustion, which can hamper our sleep patterns).

6. Go to bed only when you are tired and ready. Avoid being a slave to the clock or retiring just because your spouse is doing so.

7. Take a relaxation or visualization tape to bed with you. Some are designed specifically for sleep inducement. (Cautionary note: Do not use the same relaxation tapes you use during the day because you may begin to associate them with sleep.)

## Calming the Mind

The biggest challenge to the exercises in the previous section may be keeping your *mind* focused. In order to cope with stress overload, it is usually necessary to quiet and calm the mind as well as the body. Once again, we are talking about changing those "tapes" that play in our heads.

## Meditation

In today's world, it is most unlikely that you have escaped all exposure to this most celebrated vehicle for quieting your mind. You may, however, have encountered some misleading information about it and formed opinions based on inaccurate data. Meditation is not the province of some oddly garbed sect where devotees shave their heads and chant themselves into a trance. Nor is it part of any particular religious organization. Buddhists may meditate, but so might Protestants, Catholics, and Jews. It is not affiliated with leftist politics, vegetarianism, animal rights, or ecology movements.

Meditation is practiced all over the world by people very different from you and very like you. In the 1970s, a meditation room was established in the Pentagon so that America's top military officials could find some tranquillity and rejuvenation amid their high-stress lives. Practiced meditators find that the sense of inner peace they can reach is critical to their ability to cope when external problems threaten to overwhelm.

Research into the physical changes that occur during meditation has been going on for decades. These studies have shown that significant, observable benefits occur. For example:

- Lowered blood pressure
- Improved circulation
- Slowed respiration
- Reduction of harmful lactic acid in the body
- Slowed pulse rate

In addition, meditation produces a change in the electrical activity of the brain, as measured by an EEG. Scientists attribute this regulating effect to the feelings of inner peace that meditators describe.

Meditation can sound a lot like one more relaxation technique, but it's not. In relaxation exercises, your focus is an internal one. You observe the changes in your tension level, your breathing, and your body in general. In meditation, the focus is actually external. This may sound like a major contradiction if we are looking for *inner* peace, but by focusing on an external object, idea, or sound, without judgment or opinion, we can free our minds. That is what meditation is.

Initially, it is easy to lose concentration, and everyone does. Meditation takes much practice, and with practice it becomes easier. As you practice with some of the exercises in this section, don't "try" too hard—it defeats the purpose. When extraneous thoughts appear in your head, acknowledge them and let them float away. Just follow the instructions and see what happens, rather than trying to force it.

When you begin, it may be helpful to establish a regular time and place for meditating. This will help you form the habit. People find that meditating on an empty stomach is also helpful. Avoid alcohol and any kind of medication prior to meditating. You may find that five to ten minutes of breathing or relaxation exercises will help prepare your body for the experience.

There is quite a variety of meditation techniques. Here are two basic ones, the first of which focuses on an object, the second on a sound.

## OBJECT MEDITATION

1. Sit comfortably in a chair with your feet flat on the floor and your hands resting, open palm, on your knees. Close your eyes. Take a few deep, full breaths.
2. Think of an object. It might be a tree, a rock, a table, a vase. Hold the image of that object in your mind.
3. As other thoughts intrude, gently release them and refocus on the object.
4. Focus on the detail of the object. What shape is it? What color? What texture? Is it heavy or light? Is it firm or soft?
5. Focus all your attention on this object in your mind. Keep your focus as long as you like.

Initially it will be best to keep your meditations to ten or fifteen minutes. That may even feel lengthy to you. As you practice, you will become more comfortable meditating for longer periods of time, and you will find it easier to maintain your focus. Our next meditation involves a *mantra,* a simple sound on which to focus attention.

---

## SOUND MEDITATION

1. Choose a word or a simple sound. You may want to choose a word that has special meaning to you (e.g., *peace, truth, heal, dance, love, abundance*).
2. Sit comfortably on a chair or cross-legged on the floor. Close your eyes. Take a few full, deep breaths.
3. Begin to slowly repeat the word over and over again to yourself. You may do this aloud or in your head.
4. Be aware of the sound and feel of the word as it reverberates in your mind. Focus on the sound, rather than on the meaning. Release the meaning from your mind.
5. Continue as long as you are comfortable.

---

Many meditators practice for thirty minutes to an hour per day, and some do this twice a day. If you grow to like the meditation technique, you'll probably find that spending less than thirty minutes will feel frustratingly short. Be sure to do your meditating in a quiet place where you are unlikely to be interrupted. Get your family's agreement that no one will interrupt you for anything that isn't a dire emergency. If you live alone, turn off all distractions (TV, phone, radio).

There's really no "wrong" way to meditate, so try new techniques, listen to a tape, buy a book, take a class. The TM Institute offers classes in transcendental meditation in just about every city in the country. Once you become adept at meditating, you will find that it's wonderfully transportable. You can do it anywhere, and it's an ability you'll have for the rest of your life.

## SHARING

Healthy people who are successful at handling multiple assignments, family, career, or lots of extracurricular activities have learned to share with others their thoughts and feelings about the stressors in their lives without waiting to be asked. They talk with at least one or two trusted friends or loved ones, even if it's infrequent. The more you can disclose about your feelings and thoughts, with regard to your stressors, the more likely you will be to defuse them harmlessly. Stress is like a pressure cooker. When we share our thoughts with others, we let out a little of the built-up steam, reducing the pressure. People who lead full, hectic lives especially need a safe place to let down their guard and say whatever they think.

Those of you who already have the kind of relationship in which you feel safe in sharing this kind of information are aware of its highly special nature. It must be one in which both sides share and both sides listen—an equal partnership. It also must be one of assured confidentiality. No one wants to hear about their own problem from someone they didn't tell in the first place.

If you do not currently have a spouse or significant other or friend with whom you want to develop this kind of dialogue, you can begin to cultivate a relationship like this with someone else simply by being a willing listener. Be a sympathetic ear when someone else is upset. Notice when people look unhappy and draw them out. Not all of them will respond in kind, but it will allow you to choose from among them the person with whom you feel the most affinity. Begin slowly and test the water, then gradually increase the importance of the information you share until you are really discussing valuable and important issues and feeling good about it.

## PHYSICAL ACTIVITY

Much research was conducted during the 1970s and 1980s on the mental effects of strenuous exercise. It has been shown quite clearly that physical activity releases healing endorphins into the blood stream. Millions of Americans enjoy the benefit of unwinding after a long, stressful day by working out at a gym, jogging in the park, cycling with friends, rollerblading, or countless other activities. There are so many activities from which to choose.

No matter what your current physical condition, there is an activity in which you can participate. Choose something that suits you. Check your local YMCA or recreation department. Walk with friends at lunch. Even gardening can be tremendously therapeutic in helping to dissipate that frustration.

## TIME MANAGEMENT

Learning to use time more judiciously can help anyone lower their stress quotient. We are not born organized. Time and life management is a learned skill. Unfortunately, disorganization seems to come pretty naturally to many of us.

**We are not born organized.**

You probably adopted many of the traits and habits displayed at home when you were growing up. If your mother and/or father was organized, kept a clean house and clean children, put meals on the table with a fair degree of regularity, kept appointments, and was able to balance the family budget well enough to keep you in clothing and food, you probably learned something from them. However, in today's faster paced world, even that advantage may not be enough.

Take a time management class. If you work for a company that provides training for its employees, chances are you have access to something like that. Ask your boss what's available. If not, there are publicly offered classes in all U.S. metropolitan areas. Try your local college or even continuing education at the high school. You can also learn time management from books, and there are many of them out there. Check with your library or the biggest bookstore in town.

At a minimum, learn on your own to set priorities. Pick up a copy of Stephen Covey's wonderful book, *First Things First*. In my opinion, no one better develops the idea of prioritizing the elements of your life than he does. Discover, as you work through the exercises he describes, what is truly urgent *and* important in your life.

## PROBLEM SOLVING

Tackle the stress in your life just as you would any other problem. If solving problems is your forte (most engineers spend years perfecting this skill), use it to reduce stress as well. The basic steps to problem solving are the same, no matter where you learn it, no matter where you apply it.

1. Define the problem.
2. Analyze the causes.
3. Determine the root cause.
4. List potential solutions.
5. Select the best solution.
6. Implement the solution.

## GETTING HELP

In our "be strong . . . do it yourself" culture, no one likes to admit that he or she can't conquer the struggles and challenges of their own life. However, "help" doesn't have to mean seeing a psychiatrist. There are quite a number of other alternatives that may sound much more appealing to you. Depending on the size of the town in which you live, some or all of these options may be available to you.

## Massage

Therapeutic massage has been around for thousands of years, practiced in almost all modern countries, in various forms. In the United States today, there is a wide variety of massage techniques to sample. Swedish, Shiatsu, Reiki, Rolfing, Reflexology, and Accupressure are a few of the more popular ones being practiced today.

Massage is an excellent aid to physical and mental relaxation, especially for people who sit at computers all day or work on an assembly line. Both of these activities and others can lead to extreme muscle tension in the back, shoulders, neck, legs, and feet. Massage reduces this tension and relieves the aches and pains that repetitive motion produces.

**Human touch is a vitally important factor in our lives.**

Human touch is a vitally important factor in our lives, yet many of us go days, weeks, even months without it. When we get busy we often find ourselves too distracted for even a brief hug from someone who cares about us. One way to reduce that deprivation is through therapeutic massage.

Massage can be easily learned. There are many fine schools of massage in major metropolitan areas. Some certified massage therapists teach individual classes through park and recreation departments or YMCAs. Anyone can participate in these. It's fun and relaxing. If you are living with a significant other or spouse, you may want to learn this art together and practice on each other.

Look in your Yellow Pages, under Massage, for a clinic or individual practitioner. Both men and women practice this form of therapy, so you may choose the gender with whom you are most comfortable. Prices vary from area to area, but are usually between $40 to $75 per hour. Unfortunately, some states still have archaic laws on their books prohibiting massage being practiced as such. In those states massage therapists usually work out of chiropractic offices or health clubs. Try out several to find someone with a style you like and with whom you feel comfortable.

## Support Groups

The idea of people getting together to support one another along a difficult path stems from the phenomenal success of Alcoholics Anonymous. That organization has been around now since the 1930s, and it's bigger than ever. Other "twelve-step programs," as they are called, banked on AA's success with addicts. In addition, the medical community adopted a similar format with regard to support groups for various diseases and medical conditions.

Today, there are support groups for almost every known physical or mental condition. Some are led by counselors or therapists, others by those who have had some success in meeting their own goals and want to share that knowledge and help others. This is another area where it's wise to shop around before you make a commitment to a particular organization or group.

## Employee Assistance Programs (EAPs)

Most medium to large organizations have EAPs as part of their human resources department. They may be staffed by counselors, therapists, or registered nurses. Some are developed internally and the staff are company employees. Others are *outsourced*, meaning they are a contract service and the representative you talk to does not work for your company. In this case, the EAP office itself may be located offsite.

EAPs provide a broad range of services. They often have counseling services or support groups available on site; they make psychiatric referrals; they make medical referrals; they may have a library covering everything from substance abuse to caring for elderly parents; and they have lots of information about what is available in the community.

If you are concerned about confidentiality, by all means ask them exactly what they do with the information you give them, who has access to it, where it is filed, etc. Generally, EAPs are totally confidential whether they are an in-house or outsourced service.

## LEARNING TO LAUGH

Although I'm quite certain everyone reading this book knows how to laugh, ask yourself whether you take the opportunity to do it as often as you did before you became so stressed. I have run across some individuals who have become so caught up in their ultraserious world that they truly seem to have forgotten how.

**Laughing is good for us.**

Laughing is good for us. Medical scientists have proved this over and over. You have only to pick up Norman Vincent Peale's *Laughter Is the Best Medicine* to be convinced of its healing powers. A colleague of mine, Marianna Nunes, who has had every opportunity in life to lose her sense of humor is now a nationally recognized speaker on the topic of humor. She tells her audiences, "If you're not prepared to laugh at yourself, you're not prepared to deal successfully with the stresses of the workplace."

Find time for fun in your life. Don't buy into the idea that fun should happen spontaneously or can't be planned. Plan activities you enjoy with people you consider fun to be with. Think about those things you used to enjoy before you became so busy and build them into your schedule. I hope you're choosing ideas from this chapter based, at least partly, on whether or not they might be *fun*.

Long before he met me, my husband, who had recently moved to California to accept an engineering job, realized he wasn't having a lot of fun in his new life. Although he had a job he loved and had a good social life with many new friends, something was missing. He determined that the missing ingredient was music. Throughout high school and college, he had played in a rock band and enjoyed the variety in friends and activities that it provided. Realizing that he had abandoned music unnecessarily when he accepted his first *real* job, he sought out and found a band with whom he could play his bass guitar. Now well into his forties, he is still playing jazz and rock, still in a band, and still having fun.

**Teach your kids how to have fun.**

Decide what fun means to you and go after it. Teach your kids how to have fun. As you can see, it's one of the most valuable lessons you can give them. Teach them that being grown up doesn't mean all work and no play. Balance seriousness and laughter in your life and the lives of your family members and help everyone you know to do the same.

## FINDING THE COPING TECHNIQUE THAT'S RIGHT FOR YOU

Stress is a complex issue. Now that you understand more about it you will need to find your own path in dealing with it. No two individuals deal with it in exactly the same way, so if you find yourself getting discouraged because someone you work with is conquering his stress by cycling 100 miles per week and another colleague extols the "miracles" of yoga, remember that those are their ways of coping. You must find the way that's right for you. Whether you go it alone or through a support group, whether you make sweeping changes in your life or quiet subtle ones, whether you indulge in something offbeat or conventional, follow the path that's right for you.

# CHAPTER 10

## ASSERTING YOURSELF

**To the extent that *you* control your life, you will control the amount of stress you experience.**

Having determined your priorities, solved the problem on paper, set goals, and created some plans for yourself, you must now muster up the courage and initiative to assert your position with whoever is linked to the situation(s). That will probably mean something like saying *no* to your boss or team members about additional assignments or unloading some you've already taken on, telling your kids you're no longer available to chauffeur in the afternoons or that you won't be going to every one of your spouse's business dinners, or making phone calls of resignation to clubs or charities or professional societies.

For many of you, this may be the toughest part of the whole regimen, so pause and take the time to do some planning for this step. Based on your previous work in this book, list the actions you've decided to take and the individuals with whom you will need to communicate about it.

## ACTIONS TO TAKE

1. _____

_____

*Person(s) to Talk to About It:* _____

2. _____

_____

*Person(s) to Talk to About It:* _____

3. _____

_____

    *Person(s) to Talk to About It:* _____

4. _____

_____

    *Person(s) to Talk to About It:* _____

5. _____

_____

    *Person(s) to Talk to About It:* _____

It's critically important to position your discussion in such a way that these individuals will not feel defensive or backed into a corner. You may want to consider enlisting their help in brainstorming alternatives or ask them what they have done in similar situations. In other words, you must be clear about your intent and at the same time willing to listen to their ideas and their feelings. Be flexible during this conversation. Go into it with an open mind. One of you may come up with a win-win formula for meeting everyone's needs. *Be firm about your goal, yet flexible in considering alternative ways of reaching it.* Use this next exercise as an opportunity to plan how you will open the discussion. Use the worksheet as a guide to make as many plans as you need.

## A STRESS REDUCTION PLAN

**Plan for Discussion With:** _____

I will open the discussion by saying: _____

_____

_____

_____

_____

I will present my position by saying: _____

_____

_____

_____

_____

S/he may react by saying: _____

_____

_____

_____

_____

I will assure her/him of my flexibility with regard to how I reach my goal
by saying: _____

_____

_____

_____

_____

# REFERENCES

Byrum-Robinson, B. "Stress Management Training for the Nineties," in J. W. Pfeiffer, ed., *The 1993 Annual: Developing Human Resources*. San Diego: Pfeiffer & Co., 1993, pp. 263–284.

Covey, S. *The Seven Habits of Highly Effective People*. New York: Simon & Schuster (Fireside), 1989.

Cowley, G., M. Hager, and A. Rogers. "Dialing the Stress Meter Down." *Newsweek,* March 6, 1995.

Dunkin, A., ed. "Can Company Counselors Help You Cope?" *Business Week,* November 14, 1994.

Friedman, M., and R. Rosenman. *Type A Behavior and Your Heart*. Greenwich, Conn: Fawcett, 1994.

Gathright, A., Work Release: "Here Are Some Ways to Fight Stress at the Desk." *San Jose Mercury News,* December 29, 1993.

Gibson, V. M. "Stress in the Workplace: A Hidden Cost Factor." *HR Focus,* January 1993, p. 70.

Goliszek, A. *Breaking the Stress Habit*. Winston-Salem, N.C.: Caroline Press, 1987.

Gregory, A. "Coping Strategies: Managing Stress Successfully," in J. W. Pfeiffer, ed., *The 1992 Annual: Developing Human Resources*. San Diego: Pfeiffer & Co. 1992, pp. 9–13.

Hammonds, K. H., K. Kelly, and K. Thurston. "The New World of Work: Beyond the Buzzwords Is a Radical Redefinition of Labor." *Business Week,* October 17, 1994.

Hay, L. *You Can Heal Your Life*. Santa Monica, Cal.: Hay House, 1984.

Holmes, T., and R. Rahe. "The Social Readjustment Rating Scale." *Journal of Psychosomatic Research,* 1967: 11, pp. 213–218.

Jaffe, D. T., and C. D. Scott. *Self Renewal: High Performance in a High-Stress World.* Menlo Park, Cal.: Crisp Publications, 1994.

Kagan, N. I., H. Kagan, and M. G. Watson. "Stress Reduction in the Workplace: The Effectiveness of Psychoeducational Programs." *Journal of Counseling Psychology,* 1995:42, pp. 71–78.

Karr, A. "Labor Letter." *The Wall Street Journal,* May 7, 1991.

Keita, G. P., and S. L. Sauter (eds). *Work and Well-Being: An Agenda for the 1990s.* Washington, D.C.: American Psychological Association, 1992.

Koeske, G. F., S. A. Kirk, and R. D. Koeske. "Coping With Job Stress: Which Strategies Work Best?" *Journal of Occupational and Organizational Psychology.* Great Britain: The British Psychological Society, 1993:66, pp. 319–335.

Lakein, A. *How to Get Control of Your Time and Your Life.* New York: New American Library, 1973.

Markham, U. *Managing Stress: The Stress Survival Guide for Today.* Rockport, Mass.: Element, 1995.

Matteson, M., and J. Ivancevich. *Controlling Work Stress.* San Francisco: Jossey Bass, 1987.

Peale, N. V. *The Power of Positive Thinking.* New York: Fawcett, 1987.

Phillip, K., and K. LeGras. "Stress-Management Skills: Self-Modification for Personal Adjustment to Stress." In University Associates, ed., *The 1981 Annual Handbook for Group Facilitators.* San Diego: University Associates, 1981.

Quick, J. C., L. R. Murphy, and J. J. Hurrell, Jr. *Stress and Well-Being at Work: Assessments and Interventions for Occupa-*

*tional Mental Health.* Washington, D.C.: American Psychological Association, 1992.

Schor, J. B. *The Overworked American: The Unexpected Decline of Leisure.* New York: Basic Books, 1992.

Selye, H. *The Stress of Life.* New York: McGraw–Hill, 1976.

————. *Stress Without Distress.* New York: Signet Books, 1975.

Sinetar, M. *Elegant Choices, Healing Choices.* Mahwah, N.J.: Paulist Press, 1988.

Woods, M. "The Link Between Stress and Illness." *The Toledo Blade,* 1993.

# NOTES

# NOTES